That Something Missing

Caroline Westley

Contents

Chapter 1

At this moment, there are around 7,101,623,551 people in the world. Some are mothers and fathers, some are friends, some are happy, some are sad, and some are just trying to make it through the day. Some of these people are searching for something, a handful know what that is, others are unaware. And for some, this thought hasn't even crossed their minds. However, of the seven billion souls in the world, how many are truly satisfied, truly happy, and truly at peace with themselves?

Have you ever wondered what marks our time here in this world? Can one person and one life really make an impact on the world we live in, or is what we do irrelevant? Do the choices we make matter and affect the future? Do they really matter to us, to our lives, and to those around us?

I believe they do. I also believe that one person can impact many lives in many different ways. Some for the better, some for the worse, but we matter. What we do, what we say and how we live matters, even if we aren't always aware of this. It is true. However, to make this impact, do you need to do anything special? Or do you just need to live how you do and experience life? Do you need to be extraordinary and stand apart from the rest in some way or another? Do you need to be on television, earn millions of pounds and be known to the entire world, have two point four children, or write a book about it?

Some people naturally set out to be the best, they want to be known. Others are happy to fade into the background and just get on with what they can. Some are neither leaders nor followers. They may not be the kind of people who wish to be remembered long after they are gone. Despite being seemingly ordinary, at some point in their life, they may have had one exception: they may have saved a life, they may have married the love of their life or lived a long and happy life, content with what they have, not wishing for more. This may not be enough for some individuals, those who think they are leaders. Does this make someone memorable, or does it make them enviable?

I am where I am now, and I am the person I am today through asking these questions over the course of my short life. They have given me the understanding I need, and have shown me the person I hope to become one day.

When you are younger, it is easy for your parents, teachers and friends to tell you that you can be whoever and whatever you want. Of course, that is true, but you get to an age where you realise that people form opinions and have expectations of you. If you were bright throughout school, the general expectation would be for you to go to university and land a great job with responsibilities and a nice paycheque. If you're athletic and love playing sports, people may expect you to become a great athlete, one who reaches sporting highs. The important thing to remember though, is that you do not have a responsibility towards any one of these people; not to your teachers, your friends, and even your parents.

Yes, you will always be grateful to them for the support they have given you, but that is where it ends. You need to pursue your strengths and what makes you happy. Whatever path you choose, it should be your choice, and yours only.

The opinions and expectations of others tend to whirl round in your mind as you seek your goals. You move through life hoping to satisfy these opinions and expectations so that, one day, you can wake up to a silent mind, one with no questions. Just peace, still and quiet. Contentment. Fulfilment. I, myself, am not certain that I've managed to answer many, if any, of the questions that have been mounting up over the years, mostly formed myself, but some from other people around me. I have definitely not reached the stage of fulfilment quite yet, but it takes your experiences in life to guide you to the starting line for forming your own opinions, opinions that can lead and support you a long way down your chosen path. Everyone needs to form questions. For some, not forming and asking questions is a means of escaping the truth, not necessarily a sign of them being afraid of others lying in response. Sometimes, though, the truth is what you need to acquire fulfilment in life.

The feeling of satisfaction doesn't always arise from thoughts of your family, your friends, your job and all the things you have in your life. Everything that gives you a reason for leaving your bed every morning won't necessarily provide the comfort you need to be truly satisfied.

There are moments when you think you are practically failing in every aspect of your life. Happiness can seem as distant and unattainable as space travel, or the ability to turn back time. Moments like this may not be frequent, but they do creep up on you when you are least expecting it. You may have experienced lengthy periods of happiness, a time when you remember being satisfied, but things change, people change. Change is one of those inevitable laws of nature, exacting its toll on our lives. Mistakes are made, regrets are formed. All that remains are the repercussions, ones that make something as simple as rising from your bed seem almost unworthy and laborious.

OK, so a lot of people could ask, what more could a girl want? You have a great family, you have and have always had great friends, you have had a good education, have travelled the world and competed in sports at both national and international tournaments. You have experienced the many highs and lows that many other individuals go through throughout their lives, which inevitably leads to an accumulation of a variety of memories you would never want to lose. Like everyone else, you've had your ups and downs, now all you have to do is learn from them.

Life is a culmination of a range of events and associated feelings: there is the usual anxiety that accompanies academic exams, where you think your results are the be-all and end-all; there is the familiar rollercoaster ride that goes hand-in-hand with love and relationships, with the men or women you meet during the course of your life. Some are right, while other relationships are wrong. There are also scary moments where people close to you go through hard or sad times. But that is life, right? We all have to go through the experiences that constitute our life as we know it.

After 25 years of living, I have experienced quite a lot. Anyone who has had similar experiences to mine may wonder, what else does this girl want or expect? She is probably just being greedy. Do you know what? I agree with them. Although, I don't think I'm naturally greedy, I never really have been. I can honestly say that I would never change a thing in my life. So, why is it that I keep thinking that something is missing?

What more could I possibly expect to happen or experience that would fill this supposed gap I have? I am fortunate to have all these fantastic things, people and opportunities in my life, but somehow, I still feel as though I need that something extra, that something, whatever it may be, that will satisfy me and leave me content with life, and even myself. At this point in time, I am not in a position to answer these questions, but perhaps by the end of this book, I will be, or at least I will be closer to understanding it all. I have jumped in a little deep here by not explaining myself in the slightest. So, where do I start? When you scrutinise life, in terms of what you need and what you want, it's difficult to determine where to begin thinking about it and how you feel about it.

Chapter 2

Whenever people talk about their lives, they almost always talk about how their school years were the best years of their life. I do think most people make the mistake of wishing their school years away though, thinking of these years as being a chore and hard work, without really having the rest of their lives to compare against. It is just a fact that, no matter how many people tell you otherwise, and how many times they say it, you should cherish these years. It isn't until those early school years end that you suddenly realise, that these were the times when you learnt things, began life and formed memories.

My first real memory is of my first day at school, standing there in my new school uniform, with my new red and black backpack, looking all smart. I remember being slightly nervous, but feeling proud and excited that this was it, I was starting school, I was growing up.

It is the time when you are thrown out on your own to make friends and find your own way.

Of course it's not just you who bypasses the value of those years. Everyone in the world will recognise that at some point. They took those years for granted and flowed with the common notion that the grass is always greener on the other side, and that school was just a means to the end.

You are awoken at 8 a.m., by your mum or dad, who has breakfast ready on the table. You have to go out in the cold and be driven to school by a friend or family member. You are stuck in a classroom learning new things until 3 p.m., with play times in between. Following which, you are picked up and chauffeured home. No doubt you have some homework to do, which probably takes at least 30 minutes to complete, and then you have to pluck up the energy to think of what game to play, what book to read, or which friends to ring before having dinner and getting to bed at a decent hour for a nice long sleep, ready to start all over again the next day. You are making new friends, learning about life and discovering new concepts every day. When you look back on it now, was the grass really greener? Was it really that much of a chore to get through the week? … probably not, but you would never have thought it then.

Recently, I've had the opportunity of seeing and experiencing this life again, when seeing family members at school. The kids run into the classroom, all smiles and laughs, they play all day, come home and speak about their day only when asked. They talk about how they played with their friends, chased after girls, and read some of their new books. They moan about how they had to have a spelling test or a quiz on their times tables. But, at the end of the day, it doesn't really occur to them that they don't have a care in the world. It is the life we all wish for once we come to the end of it.

It's that time in your life where you don't think, you just do.

As you grow up, you start to wish for moments where you can have a day on your own, to relax and to think.

Although, when it is quiet and peaceful, and you're the only one about, these thoughts and feelings dominate your mind and you become totally consumed by what you believe you should be thinking, feeling and doing. Your mind can take over to the point where all your thoughts become jumbled and confused.

A lot of people go by the rule that, when you are unsure of things, or confused, you need to distance yourself and think. But, how does thinking about things actually make a difference? Thinking doesn't make things happen, so how does sitting and contemplating about things, actually make anything better? Often, the more you think, the more complicated things seem, so why not just take action. If things aren't working, do something about it, don't just sit there thinking about what you should be doing, just do it. That's exactly how we operated as children, and that is what children still do today. It seems to work fine for them. It takes us back to that age old saying about life being a journey, and that sometimes we have to just sit back and enjoy the ride.

I met some amazing people in primary school, people I could stay friends with for life. There are certain people in your life, ones you know inside out. People you know you can rely on whenever you need them, even if you haven't seen or spoken to them for years. You're confident in the knowledge that you could ring them up and ask for their help when needed. At this young age, you make friends with people because you like them and have fun together, not because you are forced to be together or because you feel it is expected of you. During our younger years, there was none of this pressure, you hung out because you wanted to, and that was it.

I was lucky enough to have a few people like this in my life, even from that early age in primary school. These people are often the most influential peers in your life. You experience so many firsts in the company of these friends: your first day out without your parents, going into town, spending your well-earned pocket money on sweets, CDs and magazines, your first trip away with the school without your parents, often your first little boyfriend, with hand holding and hugging, your first sleep over and your first exposure to those common temptations in life: smoking and alcohol. Whether you choose to become involved in these is often down to the company you keep and the path your friends help pave. From an early age, I was fortunate to have had friends who knew the difference between right and wrong. They knew the guidance their parents provided was probably given for a reason. They knew their parents were not trying to stop them from having fun. Something I wish I had taken note of when I was seven. I don't think it's measurable, but it is noticeable that your path in life, and the values you take on, have a stronger influence than you can imagine at this young age, especially by those around you. There are moments when you are faced with decisions, where you need to depend on your friends. I'm sure everyone can recall a time when they felt they needed to provide a certain answer or act in a certain way, simply because of the company they kept, and also because of what everyone else around them was either saying or doing. Some begin to feel the pressure to fit in. Well, you know you are in good company when you can look back and can say that you made the right decisions throughout your younger years. Yes, a lot of this is also guided by your family and the values you learn, which we will get on to, but the other huge influence is how you feel you have to act with your friends, how your friends behave around you and how you all work together. I could always be myself with my friends, I didn't have to change who I was and how I behaved around them. I was able to make the right decisions, but most of all, we were able to work together to make the right choices, and be confident that that was good enough.

So, we've established that primary school is pretty much a forgotten haven, encompassing a life of play, friends, and laughter, with not a worry in the world. We all recognise that it is a complete and utter shame that we cannot remember the entirety of the first seven years of our life. It's so obvious to us now, so why not then.

No matter where you come from, who your friends are, or how many you have, there are a number of common primary school experiences that we encounter, ones that can make or break us at an early age.

For instance, we all have that one friend who we met on the first day of school and stuck with throughout the remainder of our school life. We have all met the nerd of the class, the one we teased and mocked just to make ourselves feel bigger and better. There was always that strict teacher, the one nobody wanted as a teacher because we wanted an easy life, despite knowing that they were the best teacher available to provide you with a better education. And let's not forget those awkward moments at lunch tables, playtimes and on coach trips, where you needed to ensure you had someone to sit with, to show how popular you are. You have the popular group, the sporty group, and the naughty group. You have those embarrassing moments, experienced by many, and those happy memories of winning sports day, achieving the highest marks on a test or quiz, a huge achievement for yourself and those around you.

These are just some of the times that you don't really remember, but they are, in fact, some of the best moments of your life. Nowadays, when you see children enjoying their playtimes and finishing school at 3.15, having spent the duration of their day playing with friends and choosing from the best toys, you may find it upsetting that you can't remember these years clearly. Simply because, in reality, these years were amazing.

These are also just a few of the little moments that you took fairly seriously during your school years, the same moments we can now look back on and laugh about. When I think about my junior years, I realise I was extremely fortunate. I had a good education, mixed in with good times, good memories and great friends. So is there really anything here to complain about?

The process of growing up is nothing more than having to figure out which doors haven't been closed to you yet, and which ones you would like to push open. The opportunities are there for anyone brave enough to take them.

For years, your parents told you that you could be anything you wanted to be, have anything you needed and wanted, or that you could accomplish anything you put your mind to. Perhaps this is why we are so eager to grow up, to determine what potential we have and what we can make of ourselves. You're curious to find out whether what you've been told all your life really is true, and whether these opportunities exist. That is, until you get to adolescence and hit that big wall of reality.

Some may begin to realise that, actually, you don't always get everything you thought you wanted. Sometimes you get more, sometimes less, but everyone realises that it isn't as straight forward as we once thought, or hoped. You can't become pretty, smart or popular just because you want to. You don't get to sail through school and meet great friends, simply because that's what you hoped for. You may not be in a position to control your own destiny because, sometimes, you are just absorbed with trying to fit in and make it through the day, or days even.

Chapter 3

Moving onto secondary school, this is where it all really heats up. These are the years that take their toll on who you can be and who you are going to be, not on who you are right then.

It is the oldest story in the world: one day you are thirteen and planning for "someday", then all of a sudden, quietly, without you really noticing, that someday has become "today", that someday then becomes "yesterday" and so your life goes on. This is who you've become, but was this who you wanted to be?

What makes any secondary school experience so special? It's special because you do a lot of growing up there. You wish, dream and work out who you'd like to become. Secondary school is where it all happens for the first time: the heartache and the happiness, all of it. Memories of being in class and school halls will always feel like it was only yesterday, especially certain aspects of your time there. You may look around sometimes and miss its presence, trust me. But it will always be right there with you, the memories, the thoughts, and the feelings.

Again, your friends feature heavily in your secondary school life, and your life going forward. Sometimes it isn't your choice, you may have fallen in with the cool gang, the naughty gang, the swot gang, or sometimes you're merely chucked into a room, with the only option of getting on with the people there.

Usually, however, you begin to bond with people who have similar interests, similar academic levels and similar general personalities. You seek out those with compatible personas and values. You begin to form closer relationships with these people, bonding with them and trusting them. You share classes and lunchtimes, and then spend much of your time outside of school with them, strengthening that bond.

You are often defined by the group of friends you spend your time with, and this definition sticks with you all the way through those school years and beyond. For some, this can be a good thing. For others, it isn't. However, my group of friends were, and still are, the best group I could ever ask for. I was very lucky to have established myself with this group in the first year of secondary school. They were a group of people who shared a similar sense of humour and interests as myself. Needless to say, I felt very comfortable with them.

We were quite a big group of friends, which meant that all throughout my life, I always had the reassurance and comfort of having someone to talk to, someone to make me feel better when things weren't going great, or to celebrate with if things were going well.

Despite having many similarities, every one of my friends has their own niche and their own personality, which makes them special in their own way, not just to me but to all of us. Our similarities and differences contributed to the way the group fitted and worked together throughout our school life, and even now. Between us, we cover all bases, creating a striking bond that has meant that, even years after secondary school, we are still as close as ever, feeling comfortable with each other and trusting each other.

Luckily, I managed to find that circle of friends who just accept you for who you are. Everyone can be themselves and still get along. Yes, we have had our disagreements and arguments, we have moaned about each other and not spoken for a while, but that is the beauty of true friendship. Together, you experience the good and bad times, but you come out on the other side still friends and still close. During the course of my education, I always had my own interests outside of school. These kept me extremely busy and gave me little time for the usual socialising you do when you reach the age of 16 or 17. We will come onto this later. Although, limited time to get involved in activities and outings with your friends gives you the chance to broaden your perspective. You can stand back from the crowd, listen and observe. You see what people are really like, how they interact and, as you grow older, you see the greatness in each of them, and how they influenced and helped shape you into the person you are today.

Individually, each person has something great to offer. To be honest, I don't think any one of them really knows how great and special they are, nor do they realise how much they helped change and shape me.

One of them represents strength in our group. She has been through quite a few ups and downs, as have a lot of people, but even through her own bad moments, she has remained strong and you would never have known she was going through a hard time in her life. She always puts her friends and family first, regardless of her own situation. If one of us needed her, she would be there. What makes her even more special is that she doesn't realise how great she is. She is there for anyone and everyone, asks no questions and takes no compliments for this.

Another one of our group is the creator. She is one of the most imaginative and creative people I know. I knew this from when we were at school. She would doodle away during class, but she has now excelled in her career and constantly amazes me with what she does and how she succeeds.

One is the listener. This is the one who has a quieter personality, but the one who is always there to offer you a sensible, personal opinion and view, that you know comes from the heart. She is the one who is always there to listen to your problems and help you solve them. Although she is quieter and the one likely to stay in the background, I always know she will be there for me and for every one of us.

Another is the realist. This is the person who organises and brings the group down to earth. Without this person, people would be lost under the radar, we would slowly grow apart and not be as close today, as we were ten years ago. They reach for the moon and take us all along with them. They would never mind if we overtook them, as long as we remained close. The one with hidden talents is the person who has constantly amazed us with their intelligence, savvy and knowledge, but has never once behaved as though they are superior to us in any way. They are a hidden treasure and an absolute gem in our group of friends. They could do anything they put their mind to, but will always remain close by.

One is the serious person in the group, who keeps things on track but literally follows their heart, wherever that may lead them. This is the person who people secretly envy: their ability to follow a path, make mistakes, learn from these and carry on. I wish I had half the guts and strength this person must have to be able to pick themselves up and carry on as they were before. She is an inspiration.

Then there is the adventurer. She has crammed so many experiences and adventures into her life. Throughout all of these times, she maintained her loyalty, and is one of the loveliest people you could ever meet. She has learnt so much in her short life, we can count on her for any type of advice, or just a story to entertain us when we're down. Despite all her adventures, she puts her friends and family first, and is someone who will always be in all our lives.

And then there is the smiler. This person may not be the richest or the smartest, but she is amazing. However low or upset we are, however bad we're feeling, her smile and laughter has the ability to brighten our day. She is there to make us feel better whenever anyone is feeling blue. We know that, should we need her, all she has to do is smile and we're instantly better. Finally, there's me. Where and how I fit into this group, I am not sure. However, I do feel like the luckiest person when I sit back and observe the group of friends I have in my life now. I hope they stay in my life for a very long time to come.

Sometimes, no matter how hard we look, we can never see ourselves clearly.

Our own perception of ourselves is the only thing that prevents us from greater achievements. We can see our friends and family for the great and beautiful people they are, so why can't we do it to ourselves?

I'm not sure, but I do know that, whatever I do in life, whatever my ups and downs, the friends I have made will be in my life forever, to help make things better. That alone is a huge comfort and support to anyone.

There is the kind of support you ask for, the support you don't ask for, and the support that is just there. It knows when you don't want it, but shows up when you need it. This is how the friends I have are. They know me inside out and can tell when I need them. These real friends never get in my way, unless I happen to be on the way down, when they will be there to pick me up.

I think you realise you have that true friendship when the silence and stillness between you becomes complete. It is safe and easy. It's what you need in your life. I really am lucky enough to have found them.

A lot of people will be able to relate to the kind of people who form a part of my life. If you were to observe the friends you have, and the people you are closest to, you could label each one of these individuals with similar traits and personalities as I have done with my group. Some of you may have a couple of really good friends, others may have a big group, but I think if you were to stand back and look at them, think about the memories you have formed and the experiences you have been through in life, you would be able to see how great they really are.

It is hard to find people who will love you no matter what … I am fortunate to have found a bunch of them.

Friendships, however, are not immune to change. After secondary school, a group of friends may go their separate ways for a while, to follow their dreams, build their own paths and shape their lives. Some will go to university, some to find a new job, others to start a family, and some move on to other places. Each of these roads provide the opportunity to meet new people and make new friends. It is up to you to make sure your life doesn't pull you apart. My friends and I took on this challenge, and so far, we've been very successful. It is easily done where you go a week, a month, or a year without speaking. It's normal for people to have other things happening in their life. There are deadlines at work, family commitments, and the normal day-to-day responsibilities, but you have to make the effort. Sometimes it only takes a chat over a cup of coffee, afternoon shopping, or dinner, to get you back on track. These friends are the people you need in your life.

Chapter 4

University is always referred to as being some of the best years of your adult life. Although I am still only a third of the way through my life, those four years at university did change me. I had some amazing experiences and formed great memories … as would most people.

University, first and foremost, is the next academic step. It is there for people to expand and improve their knowledge, and to assist them in getting the job they want and the money they need to be able to live a secure life. Right? … Wrong.

Everyone changes once they go through university. In most instances, this is for the better. You don't just learn about your chosen degree subject, you learn about life and how to live it. It is a level of independence, where, for the first time in your life, you don't have your parents to back you up and show you how and what to do, and possibly bail you out if needed. You learn basic skills like cooking, cleaning, and budgeting. You learn how to make friends with people, who may not be the usual type of people you are attracted to. In university, you are thrown into situations where you may not be entirely comfortable. You are settled into your own accommodation and are expected to get on with others there. So you find a way because you have to. You learn to become more tolerant, more understanding, and learn that it is very rare to have any time to yourself. Life at university almost always means that there is someone around to keep you company, or just entertained. Nobody really complains of being bored at university.

But like I said, these three or four years of your life are not just about further education. People grow and change as individuals, without really noticing. Boys become men and girls become women. People grow and have the opportunity to start thinking about their future, and begin to pave the way forward. You find your strengths and your weaknesses and you begin to see the person you want to be, and the person you can be, when you set your mind to it.

Again, you form amazing friendships with people who make university life what it is. It isn't always similar to how it was at school. Sometimes you end up with friends you would never have considered being friends with, but this is what makes university life so great. It is different, it pushes you and contributes to who you are today.

I'm not going to lie, I think most parents out there would prefer to stay in the dark about what their children got up to in university. I am also quite sure that what happens there should remain a secret between you and your university. Although, they are memories that will stay with you for the rest of your life.

Anyone at the stage of considering what they should do once they finish school, needs to take a step back and visualise the bigger picture. Common paths to consider are going to university, starting a career or an apprenticeship, but there are many other paths that one may choose. There is always something more to consider. It isn't always about knowing in advance what your career goals are, or which further studies will help you most. Sometimes it's useful to gain different experiences, which could potentially open up other opportunities you could gain further knowledge from, essentially veering from your comfort zone. University offers the chance to experience many things, you can gain more than just a degree from here. To this end, I would encourage everyone, regardless of social background, academic ability, and personality type, to consider the option of going to university. It will help you grow into that person you want and hope to be.

Chapter 5

Having finished with university, what next? Where do you go from there?

When you first enter the career world, you won't necessarily be in the position you saw yourself in. It's not necessarily your final goal, or even where your strengths lie. I have come to realise two things about careers and professions.

Firstly, your working life is a long one. You work at least eight hours a day, five days a week, and for about 47 weeks of the year on average. This could go on for approximately 40 years of your life. That's over 75,000 hours of working, plenty of time to progress further. Given this length of time, why are some people so keen to start a career from an early age? Where one has to take on new responsibilities and work long hours, at an age when they could be learning and experiencing other new things or environments, before settling on a career.

People are quite keen to leave the academia and enter the world of work, but what is the rush? Yes, money is a key factor, but surely the experiences you gain from life also have significant value.

Very often, people start their careers as interns or at a junior level, a career level they most certainly do not wish to remain in for the rest of their lives. However, it is all relative. It is a learning experience nevertheless. Usually the people, who have worked in various positions, in diverse roles, or across different market sectors, are the ones who gain the most knowledge, and thus end up with the career of their choice. There is no need to feel pressurised into finding the right career, your niche. You have forty years to get there, so why rush? You have over 75,000 hours to try out different roles, learn, and ultimately settle in the position that was meant for you. Maintaining this mindset will most likely help you reach where you're meant to be. Forcing yourself into a career you believe you should be doing often results in you becoming preoccupied with meeting the goals of that role, rather than having the time to do the things you were meant to be doing, and possibly, what the world expects you to do.

The second thing I realised is that your career isn't always just about the job you do, there's much more to it.

Obviously, immediate thoughts as an employee revolve around the impact you make, the challenges you face, the things you learn and how you progress. However, I find that an occupation can be just as much about the people, as well as the environment, you work in. I haven't held a significant number of career positions, but I have experienced a few short periods of work while I was at university. I now hold a full-time job, which I've been at for about two years now. From these roles, I have experienced the value of those who work around you when it comes to contributing to your learning, your knowledge and your overall employment experience.

Whilst studying for my Masters degree, I landed my first real job. To start with, this was just a means to an end, a way of funding my education, but it created an opening for me. It was a role I could learn from. This particular role was in a professional field, one I had no previous insight or experience in. Due to this, the role was a challenge, something I wanted in my career. I have never been the kind of person who settled for something because it was the easier option, or because of my familiarity with the area, or simply because it was a role I knew I could fulfil, a comfortable role, something I could do day in, day out, with my eyes closed. I wanted something I could learn from, a job where the actions and thoughts pushed and tested my limits, and where my colleagues challenged me. I wanted to progress with the knowledge that I have worked hard. In this first job, I didn't have the background and experience needed. I was thrown in at the deep end so I could learn faster. I was also surrounded by people who'd been working in this profession for years, and I was certainly at the bottom of the pile. However, there were plenty of people around who were willing to teach me and help me learn. This alone forms a huge part of enjoying a job. Having people like these around you makes a difference because you end up spending more time with them than with your friends and families. Working with them at least eight hours a day, you get to know them inside out. If you want to feel relaxed at work and really gain something from it, it is these people you need to interact and form relationships with. Throughout a person's lifetime, they may hold several different jobs, having exposure to and interaction with many different people. At work, you have to learn to get to know people, and be able to work with people of all ages, gender, backgrounds and interests. It isn't like it was at school, or university, where people were of similar age with similar interests. There is a huge variety of people at work, and you need to be able to get on with them. You could be lucky and find someone you can relate to, or learn from. More importantly, a person you can laugh with. Let's face it, even if you have the most important or well paid job in the country, it can only be better if you have the opportunity to laugh while at work.

In the team I worked the longest with, each individual had their own strengths, which collectively made them a really pleasant group to work with. It was easy to learn from them. This is what is important to me, and to others no doubt. You want to be able to go to work knowing you will learn, and laugh.

It is great to know a person who really loves the job they do. They love coming to work, and you know they will work their hardest and do their best, simply because they love it. To work with someone like this is very uplifting. Even when you are having a bad day, that spring in their step will perk you up and get you back on track. It makes the day and week so much easier when you're in the company of someone like this. They are always ready to help you out when needed and will never take credit for your work. You won't feel like you're on your own when they are about because they will always be there to lean on and support you, whatever the issue.

You don't often meet these people, they are few and far between, but they are people who have dignity. Everyone needs someone like this in their life.

Fortunately, I also knew someone who was intelligent, hard working, committed and supportive at work. Having someone who is an encyclopaedia of knowledge, someone who is successful but down to earth and approachable, is also very rare. These are often the very experienced, and constantly busy people. Yet, they still find the time to help you out whenever you need it. This is also the kind of person who you would go out of your way to help because you know they'd do the same for you.

Trust is a big thing in any occupation. With everyone moving forward, wanting to grow and develop and "move up the ladder" as they say, having someone you trust working alongside you is a huge relief. This trust creates respect, respect forms the basis of working with, or for these individuals, much easier, rewarding and fulfilling. In my opinion, most people could probably count on one hand the number of people they can trust in their work environment. There are varying levels of trust, and it's the people who you could trust your job with, trust they'd give you credit where due, and trust that they would not take advantage, that makes work comfortable and relaxing. This eases any tensions and allows you to focus on your job to the best of your ability, then go home, leaving your work in the office.

This form of trust and respect was present in my, I suppose you could say, "superiors" at work. I have come to realise that respecting the people you work for also drives you. I have seen people who have no relationship with their boss, there is no direction, and a general lack of trust or mutual respect. Respect goes both ways, if it isn't present, there is nothing to motivate you to work harder and make a difference. Both of my superiors knew their job inside out. They both had great qualities, but were also aware of their limitations and were not afraid to admit it. Subsequently, they appreciated the work my team and I did, which made them easier to work for. Having these relationships at work are often hard to come by, but they make a huge difference. I think respect should be given no matter what responsibilities once has in their job, whether that be considered high or low, they are in a working environment. Whether you earn £100,000 or £10,000 annually, you need everyone behind you, because the higher you go, the further you have to fall. Having supportive people will not only stop you from falling, but they will help you get back up, brush yourself off and start again.

I wouldn't like to work in a role where I only put in half the effort. If I choose to do something, whether it's work, sport or just a general hobby, I want to give it my all.

Some say a job is just a way of paying the mortgage. You go to work, do your job and go home. Some people have different priorities, and I understand their way of thinking completely. Others prefer to have a job with less responsibility, something where they can leave the office at 5 p.m. and not have to think or worry about work until they return the next morning. The kind of job where you are comfortable and secure. Personally, I have always seen it as more than that, and think I always will. For me, my job should be something that drives, motivates and challenges me. Something I can be rewarded for if I do it right. The rewards aren't just financial, in the form of pay, but fulfilment when you get something right or when you complete a difficult task.

Once this fulfilment stops, I stop learning and feeling challenged. To me, this would be an indication to move on. I want something I can build on, something I can progress at. I don't want to go into an office and just feel comfortable everyday. Yes, it's nice to have those days where you know what you are doing at work, with a clear start and end, but you also want days where you aren't sure how your day will progress or whether you'll be able to complete a certain task. You know you'll be challenged by the activity, as well as the people you work with.

Your job is such a huge part of your life, something you can't run away from. You need the financial stability to live, so if you are going to commit half your life to working, surely you should try and do something that interests, challenges and fulfils you, at least most days anyway.

Again, perhaps others may think differently. There may be people who see their job purely as a means of making money. It is a means to the end, a way of putting food on the table, but that's fine. Maybe there are variables in your personal situation and family set up, which may affect your opinions on this, but for me, if I am investing my time in something, I want to do it to the best of my ability and enjoy it at the same time, if I can.

I'm sure everyone has those days when they would rather stay in bed … when that alarm goes off at 6.45 a.m., or those days where you'd rather be out in the garden when the sun is shining, rather than being stuck in a stuffy office all day. This doesn't mean you think any less of your job. Everyone has these days, but hopefully they still enjoy a small aspect of the work day once started.

When you are working closely with people, you don't just become familiar with their work life, you become a part of their overall life. You learn about their background, their family, and their social life. Some work colleagues go from being colleagues to friends.

By spending so much time with people, you learn a lot about them and see the greatness inside them. I have worked in some great teams, where I've learnt a lot about work and life in general. You learn what others have been through, the adversities they have faced, and how they have moved forward. You take these thoughts and opinions and apply them when required.

It is these types of people, people I have known for under two years, who have inspired me in more ways than one, who reinforce the importance of having work friends. They are people from different backgrounds and experiences. At work, the friends you make are different to the people you chose to be friends with, chose to spend time with and chose to share things with from your former years. You wouldn't apply and interview for a role because of the people you could potentially be working with or who you may meet. You choose a profession because of the responsibilities and opportunities it represents, and you just have to live with the people in that profession. I have always been blessed with working with people I am able to be friends with, and learn from.

There are people who are at their lowest, having been forced into this state of mind. These individuals, who you spend your eight hours a day with, are often older and wiser, with experiences you haven't faced yet. It is for this reason that you have to take the opportunity to sit and listen to them whenever possible. Even if I don't agree with a particular view, I still listen, because you never know when you may need to draw on this advice or experience. One friend in particular comes to mind, someone I've learnt a lot from in the few years I've known them. This is a person who stands apart from everyone, inspires and amazes you. When you think you are having a run of bad luck, or feel a little down, this would be the person to prop you up and make you laugh, despite having their own issues to deal with. I honestly do not think there are many people like her around. Having had a substantial run of bad luck herself, as well as her own adversity, she has fought through and maintained her positive outlook on life, and past events. She has clarity about who she is, what she wants and where she is going; she is content in herself. These traits of hers are some of the key things I have learnt, and am still learning, from her.

Perhaps it takes certain hardships to reprioritise things a little. This helps you form the clarity you need, or perhaps this is just something that comes naturally when you've accomplished what you wanted to, found a connection, and are satisfied with who you are. However, this friend of mine is a survivor, and I am very privileged to be able to learn from her daily. I may not have had the chance to have known someone like her outside of work. This is another example of the benefits of working.

People frequently moan about having to work, having to get up early, missing out on the sunny days of summer, missing out on snowball fights in winter, and generally the loss of time with loved ones. But if you think about it, if you didn't work, imagine the kind of people you'd never have had the chance to meet, the things you would never have learnt, and the experiences you would miss out on. It is one of many strands of life that exposes you to new people, new experiences, and opens your eyes to the expansive world we live in. Similarly, many people find it daunting to talk in front of an audience in a meeting room, an audience that consists of people who may have been in the profession for over 25 years. Presenting to a significantly large audience can also be daunting, but these are the experiences you take in your stride, and learn from.

Sometimes it is only the work environment that provides the opportunity to experience this.

Work, for a lot of people, is a key driver in life, where the aim is to better themselves and become something. For a lot of people, things do often go well. Your career forms a part of you and plays an important part in directing you towards things you may not have been aware of. Let's say you were out at a bar and met someone of the opposite sex. You start chatting and ask those common "get to know you" questions. If you do not have a career, a job or an interest, imagine how limited that conversation would be. It's not a person's career that defines them, but it is something that can be talked about socially, and is something that could provide valuable insights on the other person.

You can learn a lot about someone simply from how they talk about their careers. They could be a plumber, a doctor, a salesman or a teacher, but it's their passion for their job that can tell you a lot about their character.

If you cannot answer questions about what you do, what you would like to do and your general direction in life, there is a huge part of the "getting to know" someone conversation that could be missed. I know this is a simple example, but it is a relatively true one, one most people have experienced. It demonstrates the role a profession plays in forming someone. Therefore, if your professional life isn't up to expectations, it can feel as though something is missing in your life.

You are right to strive for something in your professional life and reach for success, but, as I said, it isn't just your job that has the ability to direct your path in life.

It wasn't until I was around 25-years-old that I really

started thinking about a getting job, forming a career path, and where I want to be in 20 years' time. Up to this point, I had something else driving and pushing me through life. Work formed the third chapter of my life, after my education and my sport.

Chapter 6

Sport can define a person. It certainly defined me for a large part of my life.

When you are involved in an activity, a sport or hobby, which you work hard for, commit a lot of time to, and just love doing, you begin to wonder what it would be like if you weren't playing this sport. What would happen if it was to all go away?

One of the earliest memories I have is of walking into my local leisure centre with my mum and brother. My brother went off to join the sports club my nan ran. She loved sport just as much as I did, if not more. I was left standing on the sidelines. After a bit of persuading, I was allowed to join the same club, despite being too young, and I never looked back.

When you are young, I don't think you ever know why you become interested in a particular sport. All activities are fun, exciting and energetic. You just want to take part in everything, run around and have a good time with your friends. If you are the sporty kind of person who loves taking part, you begin to gain a level of competitiveness, where you not only want to take part, but also have the desire to win. You can't help it, it becomes natural to you and it sticks.

There are a lot of people who often find themselves drawn to something unintentionally.

Sports must run in my blood. With my whole family having played the same sport at some point in their life, at varying levels, it was natural for me to want to continue this trend. Especially as I had the natural ability, something that I may have acquired from my family. It was inevitable. Love of sports had been in my family for three generations, so I don't think I would have ever made it through life without considering sport, and loving every moment of it.

I started playing when I was young, aged seven or eight. Seeing my brother and cousins enjoy playing in junior clubs meant I couldn't wait to join the club. From the moment I started playing sports, in school and out, I loved it. I loved the feeling of running free. I loved the competition and loved the desire and need to win. As I grew up, I became more heavily involved and trained hard every day. I began to fall in love with that feeling where you push your body, and yourself, to the limit; that feeling of pain, which I can only describe as "good pain" and "satisfying pain", when you know the pain is temporary, but will only help you later. It comes back to the well known sporting quote that most athletes try to remember when they're in the middle of a tough training session: "Pain is temporary, winning lasts forever". Although, when you're out on a ten mile run at the crack of dawn in the middle of winter, with your body aching and freezing, you're hardly in a position to say you love and enjoy it. You know, though, the feeling of pushing your body further, the feeling when you finish, knowing you've pushed your body to accomplish something, will only make you feel better.

When you find a passion, or love, like this, you don't

need easy, you just need things to be possible, and that's how you want to continue.

It isn't just the competition that people fall in love with, they fall in love with the training, the dedication and the challenge that comes with a sport. Some people don't understand it, but I do.

When you are running along the road, it doesn't matter what you look like. Whether you have trendy clothes on, whether your hair and make-up is perfect, it really doesn't matter. The road doesn't care what job you have, what social class you are or how far you will run. The road won't judge you. It allows you to be who you want to be, lets you think about whatever you want, and lets you do what you want. The feeling you get is like nothing else. It's sort of rare to be able to experience this mindset. From my perspective, I'm very glad I have this thought process built into me. Having an older brother, who also loved sport, gave me more of a competitive streak. Having him there pushed me and created the healthy competitiveness we both needed to stand out and be the best. Although, in my eyes, I never won. However, this streak has only grown since.

I became involved in a variety of sports during my school years. From one sport to another, that competitiveness never faltered. Whether I was playing in the school netball or basketball team, doing cross country in P.E class, or doing gymnastics and playing in badminton competitions at a high level, I always wanted to win and was committed to working as hard as I could to try and be the best I could. Second place was never enough for me, that was obvious from an early age. I think some people are just born with an enthusiasm for competitive sport, where they can work hard and be the best. It's quite possible all athletes across the world, both male and female, must have had the mental capacity to form the strength and dedication to have the willingness and power to do what it takes to become the best. Without strength and dedication, chances of competing at a high level would be slim. This was clear to me from an early age, and gave me a necessary, but amazing, work ethic that has stuck with me throughout my life.

Actually, it's good that not everyone is like this when it comes to sport. Sport can be a game, a hobby, pure exercise, recreational or competitive. The common factor, regardless of the level you take it to, is that sport is fun. For sport to continue growing, and to keep people active, it's good for everyone's perspective on sport to vary. Sports are there to highlight that you don't need to be the best to take part. So it's a good thing that not everyone has a similar mindset to myself. There are various perspectives on how sports have affected my life. My work ethic did drive me to train harder. It also taught me to really push myself and make a career out of my sport. I want to try and take it to that next step where it is no longer just a hobby but a profession, a career and a way of life.

Sport gave me a focus and commitment that could be used in many aspects of my life, and for that I would never change anything. It has opened up so many doors for me and given me so many experiences that, despite the pain and disappointment, it has supported me throughout my career. I would never do anything any different.

It has made me believe that, at their best, athletes and many sports can be transcendent. It reminds us that an underdog can still find glory. Sports don't label people, it doesn't discriminate because of race, weight or looks. Sport can show you that there may still be magic in this world. It changes your thoughts, habits and your way of life, often without you even realising it.

By training hard daily, and pushing myself to limits I never knew I could achieve, I have had the opportunity to travel the world, meet some amazing people, who will be in my life forever, people who have helped create some of the greatest memories. Inspiration comes from the people around you when you are pushing the limits every day. Obviously your family and friends are important, but you form a relationship with the coaches who help you reach your goals. It has to be a relationship based on trust, loyalty and admiration. If those factors are not there, it could be difficult for the coach to influence your career in a way that is needed for you to move to the next level. That is what a coach does, they push you further when you think you have reached your limit. You need to trust them to know your limits better than yourself. It is an intense relationship, which can be very confusing and complicated, but it is a relationship that can overcome a number of obstacles, as long as you communicate and trust each other.

Relationships will vary with each of your coaches. Fortunately for me, my dad coached me all the way through my sporting career, allowing me to trust that, from the start, he knew what was best, simply because he was my dad, one of the only two people in the world who truly understood me. My dad demonstrated his belief in me through committing the time and effort to my badminton practices. He gave me the motivation to train my hardest and play to the best of my ability. He also never lost the main objective of the sport, which was for me to enjoy what I was doing. However well I played, however far I reached in the competition and whoever I lost to, my dad always brought me down to earth … he reminded me that I had to enjoy what I was doing. This, I am sure, is why I have continued to love the sport so much. I had another two coaches who helped me compete at the level I did. The first coach taught me basic skills and continued to show me how to enjoy the game. The second one pushed me beyond my limits. I often believed this second coach was the bad guy. I'm certain I spent the majority of my training sessions hating him because of the intense training he put my body through, and the fact that he never let me quit. In reality though, this is a typical relationship you would have with a coach. However, you should be able to trust your coach to be aware that, although you are hurting and your body is screaming for you to stop, the coach knows the training will help you move forward … and so do you.

These individuals may not be family, but they influence your life more than you think. By training you, they continue to instil a focus and dedication, the ethics of hard work and the persistence to get something right. There are many skills you gain, that not only relate to sport, but also help you through life. It's not necessarily something you will realise straight away.

Of course, you're bound to argue with your coach. You have those days where you really don't agree with a training session, where your coach shouts at you to move faster or hit harder when your body honestly feels like it cannot do anymore. This is typically the complicated nature of the bond of a coach and a player. My two coaches and my dad taught, pushed and inspired me. Their belief in me was more than I could ask for. It helped me to get to where I have with my sport, but also outside of sport. Possibly unknowingly, they helped me map my life without the need for me to verbalise my desires.

I once read an inspirational book whilst I was training and competing at a relatively good level. The author had researched outliers in their field of sport, great athletes, great musicians, famous artists or inventors. There was also a focus on children and adults who had excelled in their careers or professions, whatever that may be. The book attempted to look at what made these individuals exceptional, what distinguished them from the rest of the population, thereby labelling them as outstanding, placing them in the "outlier" category.

It also discussed how athletes, musicians, artists, and many other professionals clearly required a natural talent and dedication to succeed in their chosen path. Importantly, it stated the need to have at least 10,000 hours of practice under your belt to take your talent to extraordinary levels. The author detailed cases of players who practiced for that extra half an hour a day, or those extra few hours a week, in order to visibly progress and reach higher limits from an earlier age. These are the ones who went on to become outliers in their chosen career or profession.

My personality naturally pushed me to strive for the best, it drove me to excel, and helped me do the training; pushing myself to work hard was never a problem. My coaches said, and my parents agreed, that pushing me to do the work wasn't an issue, it was holding me back from not pushing myself too far that was. They often saw me push myself too far. Turning up for training when my body was so tired, and trying to fit in work and my studies as well, made me so tired, I became ill.

Looking back, perhaps I was responsible for pushing myself too hard during training, causing injuries that could have been avoided if I had taken things a little easier. I always thought an injury meant I'd hit the limits my body was willing to reach. Although this is a different perspective, and perhaps a wrong one, it's what helped me get to the heights I reached, of which I have to be really proud.

Of course, there are times when you wake up and are reluctant to push yourself. You sometimes wish that you didn't dream of being that one in a million superhuman, striving for something difficult, but something perhaps a little more attainable. Most likely though, your love for what you do, and the enjoyment it brings, will drown out those thoughts and let you continue your journey towards your goal. You know this goal will be difficult to achieve, and that it's a long shot, but this won't deter you. That's all you need to be a champion.

Chapter 7

This is what I'm like. It's a habit and way of thinking that I've found hard to get out of. If I'm honest, I will probably always be one of those people who are unable to sit still, always needing to be busy, moving forward, and achieving. For reasons unknown, this is just me.

Although this may sound like a good trait to have, not knowing your limits and pushing yourself too far does have its downsides.

At the age of 16, I broke my ankle in a competition. Unwilling to stop, I had it taped up and tried to continue the game. I ended up with a broken ankle and two torn ligaments. I was in a plaster cast for eight weeks and it took me out of competitions for six to nine months. However, during this time, I remember going down to the local leisure centre with my dad, sitting on a chair, and continued training with my good leg. Later, I carried on on my crutches, going along to the gym and exercising as much as possible. I couldn't stop myself. I just couldn't sit around doing nothing for eight weeks, knowing that, had I still been in the competition, I would have been training hard and improving, even if I was just standing still.

At 20, I had pushed my body to the point where my

right knee gave up on me. I needed surgery to continue with my sporting career. At that point, I wasn't ready to give up on my dreams and hopes of competing at a higher level, so I opted to have the operation. I'm not sure if it was the competitor in me not wanting to quit, or whether it was the hope and positive thinking that my injury would be fixed enough for me to compete, but I knew I wasn't ready to stop something that formed such a huge part of my life. I couldn't stop. As I said before, no one has ever had to push me to practice and train, it was quite the opposite, people tried to stop me from going too far. I returned to playing too soon, tried to train too much too early on. I was desperate to play and improve again, to reach the standard I wanted. This meant more problems with my knee, which held me back further, but I was determined not to let my knee injury impact my career. Ultimately, I think I learnt to cope with the discomfort when I played, highlighting how determined I was to not stop playing before I'd reached my peak and was ready to stop. I somehow found a way to ignore the discomfort and took it as a normal aspect of my sporting life. I got used it I suppose.

I talk about this as though I'm the only person in the world who has experienced this, but that couldn't be further from the truth. There are millions of people in the world who are dealing with much harder things than I've had to deal with on a daily basis. When I talk about my experience, and how upset I was that I would have to end something I loved doing, I feel quite embarrassed. In these circumstances, when something is taken away from you, something that means everything to you, it feels like it's all about yourself. Although, it's not, is it? As I said at the start, there are 7,061,182,591 people in the world, and I am just one of them who's trying to pursue something that actually may not be my destiny. People have been through, and will go through worse, but at that moment in time, you just do not have the perspective. Sometimes you get so caught up in your hourly and daily routine of life, you never get the chance to step back and see the bigger picture.

At 24, I pushed my body too far again during training and managed to break my foot whilst on a training run. Another six months out of play.

At 25, I spent my Christmas and New Year break training hard, ready to compete in a run of tournaments in January, that would lead on to the senior national championships. During the first competition of the year, and in my third match, I managed to dislocate my knee, rupturing ligaments and tearing cartilage in the process.

I know I am biased, but in my opinion, there was no fairness in this whatsoever. I worked and trained hard, and took my sport seriously, with a passion to succeed. Would it be considered fair that the person who'd probably trained the most over that holiday period then sustains another injury? No probably not, but is anything really fair in anyone's life?

I know injury comes part and parcel with any sport. All athletes experience some form of injury at some point, an experience that is supposed make you stronger and give you character. It is said that athletic people who go through adversity, like a major injury or illness, bounce back better and stronger, with a renewed passion for their sport, and the desire to push harder and faster. How many times must one be knocked back before they start seriously thinking, "Am I chasing the right dream?"

I asked myself that question many a time, during

injuries, during defeat, or when I was only halfway through a three hour training session and my body was already in pain. But who wouldn't think that when their body was crying out for rest and you still had an hour of intense training left with no break? Who in their right mind would think this was truly what they were supposed to be doing? But you carry on because, without a dream and a goal to chase, that something you think is missing grows bigger, and it will keep on growing until you lose sight of what you are chasing and your goals. Everyone needs that dream to chase, or that hope, because otherwise, you will find yourself lost, with no direction, and that isn't a nice place to be.

Chapter 8

Many people often ask themselves, "What if I can't do it?"

In my opinion, the question they should be asking is, "What if I can do this?" Thinking positively about that one thing that you are working towards, could actually mean you succeed in this. You should be considering what next steps to take when you succeed, not if you fail.

Henry Ford once said, "If you think you can do something, or think you can't do something, you're right".

To be able to move forward, your thoughts should be centred on the fact you can succeed. This is one attribute that each of the outliers or champions mentioned earlier would have in common. They know they can succeed, and they believe they can be the best. Whenever you hear an outlier in sports, literature, or music, talk about their career, they almost always mention a time when they didn't think they would succeed. Instead of going with this, they turned this around and came back stronger than ever. You need this confidence in yourself to find that something in life that can make you happy.

The famous Muhammad Ali once said that, "Champions aren't made in gyms. Champions are made from something they have deep inside them: a desire, a dream, a vision. They have the skill and the will. But the will must be stronger than the skill".

It's true that obstacles shouldn't form a barrier to reaching your goal. If a champion was to run into a wall, they wouldn't turn around and give up, instead they would find a way to climb it, pass through it, or work round it because that's how champions operate.

Sport is more than just a form of exercise that people take up. Sport makes people champions. These individuals go further than others and push beyond what they think possible. That's what makes someone great, someone like Muhammad Ali.

So after all the pain, sweat and tears from chasing your goal, what happens when the decision is taken out of your hands, when your dream of 15 years, the dream you committed yourself to, the one you made sacrifices for, is taken away from you? Without permission, without a warning, it's gone. What happens next?

I am an athlete, that's what I am. Sometimes merely thinking and saying this sentence over and over throughout your life could make you both believe in it and that you can be this for as long as you want. But this doesn't always work out.

How do you face living a life that is so different to what you would have chosen? How easy is it to give up on a dream you may have had all your life after being told that it is no longer the way forward for you?

I've always been of the thought that if, after trying my hardest and doing as much as possible, I didn't make it to the dizzy heights I was hoping for, then I would be fine. On the other hand, if I woke up one morning in the future, knowing I hadn't done everything I could, then I would regret it … and I don't want any regrets. It's rare for anyone not to have some form of regret though. The key is to avoid forming regrets in the first place, but if you do face them, do not let them interfere with your current state of happiness, or restrict your future through interfering with your motivation to move forward. Use these regrets as something to learn from.

We spend so much of our time wishing, wanting, and pursuing, but that is good. Ambition is good, as is hope. It's good to have a dream, and it's also good to chase goals that maintain your integrity. However, if you could turn back the hands of time, if you knew you'd see a particular friend again, what would you say to them? If you could do one last thing for someone, what would it be? Would it be something that you may have regretted in the past? Something that has prevented you from gaining that coveted title of happy or satisfied?

You should always hold on to the belief that you can make a wish, place it in your heart, and it will come true. This could be for anything you've wanted or hoped for.

You never know when the next miracle, the next memory, the next smile will come, or when the next wish will come true. Though sometimes, if you believe that a miracle is right around the corner, and you open your heart and mind to the possibility of it, and even to the certainty of it, you just might get what you wished for.

The world is full of magic. Perhaps we just need to tap into it and have trust. We may not understand it, we may not see it, but we must believe in it.

So make a wish and believe with all your heart. That is all you can do.

Often you pray or wish for something and that wish comes true. Does this mean it was a magical coincidence, or is it a consequence of the process of just being aware of what you want and seeking it?

Is a prayer the same as a spell? Could they essentially be similar in that both would keep your desires at the forefront of your mind, and potentially feed into your hands for you to grab and run with?

I think that desire, spells and prayers are all similar. When you pray, you pray for something. It's the first step towards acknowledging that you want something, that you long for it. Often, unknowingly, this can be the hardest thing to do. It takes courage to identify what you really want and desire. Courage gives you the strength to acknowledge that you are unhappy without this, and you may carry on being unhappy. Perhaps you don't need to pray or wish, but you need to acknowledge the sorrow of what's missing in your life. You need to find the courage to recognise your mistakes and what you need to do to re-establish happiness.

In a way, magic is the act of making a wish come to life. Exerting your will to the world can sometimes make something happen. So perhaps we all have that magic within us, but we really need to look for it.

Someone once told me that you have to create your future from the future, not the past. You mustn't forget what has occurred; it was a huge and important part of your life, but you need to move forward and search for the next chapter, the next opportunity, or the next love of your life. You'll never forget your first love. For me, sport was, and will always be, my first love. At some point though, you have to put that first love aside and search for something new to love with the same intensity … well, nearly as much anyway. You take what you've learnt and run with it, but try and find something else to fill that gap.

Chapter 9

So your dream has gone … do you have to come up with a new one, a new goal? Or can you carry on with life to see where you end up and what you end up doing? If you don't think you'll reach where you were planning to be for the past 15 years, then do you need a plan B?

There are moments in our lives when we find ourselves at a crossroad, afraid, confused and without a roadmap. The choices we make at moments like these can define the rest of our life.

Choices are the building blocks of our lives. They define you and what you do, with new choices available daily. You must face these and take what you have learnt from yourself and others around you to make the right decisions for you. This can be hard, but if you do not make these choices, you don't learn, forfeiting the chance to live the life you wanted or hoped for.

I believe life is about timing, opportunities and choices. Sometimes the opportunity presents itself at a time when you're ready to make the right choice. You just need to step up and take it.

Of course, when faced with the unknown, and potentially

future impacting choices, most of us prefer to turn around and revert to the known. However, it's only when you're tested with these difficult choices and unfamiliar opportunities that you truly discover who you are and the potential you have. This is the time when you discover who you can be now, and in the future.

You begin to focus on the person that you want to be because you know that person does exist. They exist somewhere on the other side of the hard work and faith you put into yourself when working towards this goal, eliminating the fear of the unknown.

I know there is life after sport, and there is life without sport. There are only a handful of people in the world who continue their sport as a career and profession. They are the lucky few, who are able to wake up every morning and do the things they really love. They are able to place all their focus, attention and effort into their passion, without feeling guilty about forgetting other aspects of their life. When you look at some of these people though, it's clear that some take this liberty for granted. A part of my life was like that, where I focused on making the most of my talent, but that freedom didn't last. It's only when I woke up one day and wasn't able to spend as much time on my passion that I realised what a blessing it was.

You want to wake up every morning with a passion. You want to wake up with a smile on your face because you love what you do. You can dream about this lifestyle, or you can go out and make it happen.

The crossroads where important decisions are made can help pave your life, what you will do with it and what you become.

When I had my sport, my first real love, taken away from me, it was upsetting, frustrating and felt unfair. A large part of how I felt had to do with the control being taken away from me. I wanted to be the one to decide when to stop playing. I wanted to do this when I'd reached my peak and chosen not to sacrifice any more for my sport. The ability to make this decision was taken away, and that was half the frustration. I couldn't train, or even exercise, because of my injury. It has been said that we don't realise the significance of certain moments of our lives until the moment has passed. We grow complacent with ideas, things or people, and we take them for granted. It's usually not until you lose something, or are about to lose something, that you realise how wrong you were, how much you needed it, and how much you really loved it.

Letting go is never easy. As athletes, we have an expiration date. Even if we are lucky enough to have a substantially lengthy professional career, or even just a prolonged go at it, that expiration date can come pretty early for some of us, sneaking up and taking over without you even realising it. Sometimes our hearts can be willing, but our bodies fight against it. That's what happened in my case.

I was in full control of my sport. It was up to me how much I trained, how often I exercised and how hard I worked. If I wanted to get up at 6 a.m. to practice before school or work, I could. If I wanted to stay in bed and forget training, then it was down to me if I then lost in the next competition. Exercise and sport was my outlet. If I was upset, annoyed, frustrated, I would go to the gym, go for a run, or take my anger out through exercise. To have that taken away from me didn't seem fair.

When something you were great at, something you loved, comes to an end, you do wonder whether you'll be good at another thing in future.

When I think about it, I wonder if I failed because I wasn't sure whether it was the fact that I couldn't do the thing I loved, or whether it was the loss of control of being able to make those decisions and not reaching my potential. I hadn't reached my goal or completed what I had set out to do. To me, that made me a failure. I'm not saying that I was the best, and I am not naïve enough to think that I could have been one of the best in the world. All I am saying is that I felt there was more to give and experience from this part of my life before I had to stop, but it was cut short and there was nothing I could do about it.

It was my passion. It was my dream. It was me. All of the sacrifice and pain would have been worth it if I had been given the chance to reach the point of my capacity. I could have worked towards reaching this peak, which would have made a huge impact on my life and sent me along a different path.

If hard work mattered, then I would have made it. But it doesn't always, and I damn well wish it did.

Chapter 10

Chinese proverbs are striking in their belief that hard work and self reliance will, in time, bring recompense.

It is known that workers in Chinese rice paddies often use the saying, "*No one who can rise before dawn three hundred and sixty days a year fails to make his family rich*". This seems totally unreasonable and unthinkable to most, but this belief in hard work ought to be a thing of beauty, and that is how I see it. Many success stories involve, along with other variables, someone or a group working harder than their peers; working longer than what others think is realistically possible.

People often think that being good at a subject, a sport, or a hobby requires an innate ability … you either have it or you don't. But sometimes attitude plays a large part. Being naturally able is a key factor, but you also master something if you are willing to try. Success is often the outcome of persistence, doggedness and the willingness to work hard for something where a lot of people would give up quickly.

Some succeed because they are destined to, but most succeed because they are determined.

Through observing our own lives, and the lives of friends and family, it's clear that success often follows a predictable course. It's not always the brightest who succeed. Neither is success simply the sum of the decisions and efforts we make for ourselves. Instead, it is a gift. It is about being given opportunities, and individuals who have the strength and presence of mind to seize and run with them. Certain people can pinpoint when an opportunity arose and was seized. These are the moments in your life that determine who you are going to be. They may not always be obvious, but they are key moments in your life. It could be as simple as being born at the right time, to the right parents, in the right location, and in the right culture. Often they are moments and opportunities you are unable to directly influence, but there is an element you can control.

Learning from both positive and negative choices can be a simple task, but it's amazing how often they are overlooked.

We are often so caught up in the myths, ideologies and beliefs of the best, the brightest and the self-made, that we seem to succeed at times. We believe that these outliers spring naturally from the centre of the earth. We look at some of these amazing individuals, who become immensely successful, and marvel at them. But surely this is the wrong lesson to be teaching others, as well as believing ourselves. Life gave these individuals the opportunities to build on. Surely, to build better lives, we need to stop focusing on this patchwork of lucky breaks and arbitrary advantages that a specific number of individuals have, which can influence and determine success, and move towards something that can provide opportunities for all. It is up to each individual to take advantage of any openings and breaks. Many outliers will admit that they were lucky in life. Not many would say, "I did this by myself". Whether they be top-performing athletes, musicians, or academics, their success isn't just down to being exceptional, it is a mixture of a web of luck, advantages and inheritances. Some of these are earned, some are passed down, some are deserved; all are critical in making a person who they are.

Success in their field is what everyone dreams about. We all want to be the best, to reach our peak, and succeed. I don't think anyone can deny this.

There are, however, some things that success is definitely not. Success can't be measured by fame, power or money. It can't be determined from one having the biggest house or the most attractive partner. Success, to me, is waking up in the morning, excited and happy about what you have in your life and what lies ahead, literally making you jump out of bed.

It could be working with people you love and look up to, or connecting with people around you, that can make a difference, in ways you sometimes don't even notice. You want to make people feel inspired and comforted. When all this is done, success for me would be falling asleep at night knowing I have done all that I could, having done the best job possible.

Looking back on what I have worked for and thought about over the years, all the hopes and dreams I had, I've come to the conclusion that, if things had turned out the way I wanted, it would be a measure of a successful life. Some would say I'd failed though. I actually think that these people, ones who do not even try to reach a goal, are the ones who have truly failed. People who don't put themselves out there, who are more scared of failure than success.

We often believe that success is exclusively a matter of individual merit, but there is very little in any the history of career tycoons and technology greats to suggest that things are that simple. These stories, instead, are about those who were given a special opportunity to work really hard, and they seized it. This happened to come of age at a time when that extraordinary effort was rewarded by the rest of society. Success isn't just of your own making, it is also a product of the world, the times you live in, and grow up with. Therefore, this is not always within your control.

Bill Gates grew up in a time where computers were just materialising. So with his immense interest in IT and his opportunity to learn with friends and family, success came hand-in-hand. That's not to say that he wouldn't have worked for every penny he earned, and that there weren't hours and hours of practice and effort. Timing still played a huge part in his success.

Some are afraid of failure. Subsequently, they're reluctant to put themselves out there, in an attempt to reach their dreams. There is no shame in being afraid. Everyone is afraid of something, but for some, that may result in failure. One needs to figure out what they're afraid of. When you put a face to fear, you can use it and beat it. I don't like failure, in any aspect of my life, but I can always say that I tried. I had a goal and I worked my damned hardest to try and achieve it. If that is failure, I'm OK with that, and I can continue happy with the knowledge of what I have done.

Going back to the book I alluded to earlier, where I discussed talent and outliers, was injury and adversity incorporated into the path to becoming outstanding? Alongside natural talent, the determination, and those

10,000 hours of practice, was luck built into the story?

I think luck has a bigger part to play in your road to becoming exceptional, more than any other aspect. You might have a natural ability, you might train harder and practice more than anyone, but if luck isn't on your side, you have no chance. Luck definitely wasn't on my side. However, luck is different to opportunity. Lucky is winning the lottery. It is something that has taken little work to achieve. It is miles different to being given an opportunity and seizing it. Opportunity is a situation that is favourable towards attaining a goal. It also forms a good basis for advancement or success. Opportunity is more about taking advantage of the circumstances that come your way.

The word luck often fails to capture the work, the effort, the imagination, and the acting on opportunities, that are often hidden behind success.

I suppose some may call it luck, but perhaps fate is a better word for it.

Is this fate? Is "fate" actually real?

A lot of people discuss it in terms of certain people, activities or events, which places them on a certain path, one that was always paved out for them. A path that leads to somewhere you are supposed to be, or someone you are supposed to be with. Some people do not believe there is such a pull in our lives, and that it is up to us where we go and what we do. Although, fate is a term that can be thrown about a lot, without a true understanding of its influence on our lives.

Fate, I believe, is something ultimate, something written in stone. To us, it is vague and unknown. It is near impossible to figure out what it is exactly and where it can take you. It is something you have no control over, and therefore, something you cannot improve, alter or influence.

Destiny, however, is completely up to you. It is in the choices you make, the journeys you take, and the dreams you chase. What becomes of you is totally up to you.

However, as much as I would like to believe that we are the master of our destiny, it has been acknowledged and proved that other variables have a far greater influence on who we are and what we become. Something we really cannot control.

There are some who say our destiny is tied to the world we live in and the land we live on. It is as much a part of us, as we are of it.

There are others who say fate is woven together so that our destinies are intertwined with so many others.

Our destiny and hope is the one thing we search for and fight hard to change.

Some never find it, others are led towards it.

There are some who say that fate is beyond our command, but I think I know better.

I think our destiny is within us. It just takes courage. You just have to be brave enough to know what you want, recognise it and seize it.

So that marks the end of that chapter of my life.

I had a dream I was chasing, but fate felt that there was something different, something bigger and better perhaps, something more suited for me or the people around me. Perhaps there is something else that I am supposed to do. That may be the reason my sports dream ended, forcing me to find a new path, and something else to be successful at.

It was a huge chapter, one I dedicated a lot of time, thought and effort to, but perhaps there is something bigger and better waiting. I can only wait and see.

Sometimes you don't want to let go of your old dreams. Dreams you've worked towards for most of your childhood and adult life, something you may have dedicated hours, days, months or even years of your life to. Despite this, sometimes your only choice is to close that chapter and start writing a new one. You find something else to focus on, to commit to, and you start dreaming about what that may turn into and where that could take you in the future.

You work as hard as you can to get something or somewhere. If you wake up one day and you aren't where you want be, or certain events got in the way, preventing you from reaching your target, your only regret would really be in the knowledge that you could have done more. If I could have worked and tried harder, or trained more, I would have been disappointed. By working my hardest, knowing there wasn't much more I could have done, I can be satisfied with where I got to.

Some people barely come within touching distance of their dreams. They don't get to experience that feeling and never find out how it feels to do what they love for a living, every day. It can be tragic when something tough is taken away from you, but the true tragedy is when you lie awake wondering, "What if?" In this situation, it's normal to be frightened of what comes next, but you shouldn't be. Embrace the uncertainty and let it take you places.

Be brave as you face life's challenges. Ones where you exercise both your heart and mind on your journey towards creating that new path to your new goal. Hopefully this will result in happiness and satisfaction, with little time wasted on regret.

If you've done all you can towards your dream and goal, regret has no place in your thoughts and in the actions that follow.

Spin wildly into your next move. Enjoy the present and each moment as it comes. You may relive these moments again. If there's ever a time when you look up and find yourself lost, simply take a breath and think about your achievements and where you are right at that moment. Think about your hopes and you will find your way again, following that new path to that new dream. It's the only mindset to be in when searching for that ultimate happiness and contentment.

So make a wish, wish for anything and everything you want. Believe it can come true. You never know when and where the next miracle will come from. If you let yourself believe that it is right around the corner, open your heart and mind to the possibility and serenity. Your wish might just come true. Perhaps the world is full of magic; we just need to believe in it, and things may just go right for you.

With this in mind, I say goodbye to that chapter of my life. However, I will continue to look forward to what comes next.

Although things didn't work out for me, I can honestly say I love sport, all sport.

It teaches you lessons that are rarely learnt elsewhere: not through school, through university, or from family. Had it not been for sports, I would have been a different person. It's similar to having many skills, hobbies and talents, which come from life's experiences. Sport taught me about maturity, commitment, hard work and discipline. Alongside this, it taught me to aim high, aim to win, and how to cope with loss. So whenever I felt that there was something missing, or I air the moon, my life in sport influenced my response to these feelings. Has sport made me want to strive for more, to never be happy being average or second best? Perhaps it has. This lesson seeped from my sports life and into most aspects of my life. I wouldn't be happy with a pass mark on an exam, I would want a merit pass. I wouldn't be happy with writing an average report at work either, I'd want it to be excellent and praised.

Chapter 11

So yes, although things didn't work out in terms of a sporting career, I would not change a thing … and God, I still love sport.

Sport can bring out the greatness within us. On any given day, it is possible for an underdog to rise up and surprise us all. Everyone has the opportunity to demonstrate their personal qualities such as strength, teamwork and dedication. Knowing we possess greatness within us gives one hope and faith, and we can achieve anything we put our minds to.

A lot of people have the mindset that the sky is the limit and there is no need to settle for second best. If everyone sat down for a day and truly thought about what they wanted as they were growing up, where they were now, and what could have been, would everyone be like me and think there was something missing all along. People go about their day, school, work, family, but never take the time to think,

"Is this what I wanted?

Is this what I want?"

If you were to look back on your life so far, would you be happy with what you have tried, accomplished and produced?

The question you have to ask yourself is: What would be the measure of life? Is it defined by the people we choose to love? Or is it simply measured by our accomplishments? And what if we fail or are never truly loved? What then? Can we ever measure up? Or will the quiet desperation of a life gone by drive us mad?

Chapter 12

It is often a fact that we strive for the best and look for the wrong things in life: the actions, materials or status we think will make us happy. We want the most money, the most expensive car or the biggest house in the neighbourhood, but are these really the things that make a difference in our lives, or make us truly happy for a larger part of life, rather than just placing a smile on our faces for a day or two. Throughout life, we often take friendships, love and family for granted. We assume they will all fall into place and that things will work themselves out. We don't spend much time thinking about improving these relationships, investing time in them, or thoroughly enjoy the time we have with our loved ones. But perhaps we should focus more on these relationships and work harder to understand, truly enjoy and make the most of our lives. These are the things that really matter; the things that will surely bring us happiness.

The way one focuses on relationships is dependant on personality, which itself is influenced by many factors in life, such as the people you meet, adventures you take or events you are part of. The greatest influence, however, are the choices you make along the way.

I have had the opportunity of meeting many different people, from different countries, cultures, generations and backgrounds. By talking to these people and being exposed to their varying personalities, I have had the opportunity to experience the obvious variations in perspective, in terms of what they want from life, what would make them happy, and what they would consider an accomplishment in life. Some people are content with what they have and want nothing more. But are they untruthful to me, or to themselves rather? Personality plays a large part in regard to whether people have the desire to strive for more, work hard to achieve this, and immediately strive for more without taking the time to reflect on their achievements to date. Most people rarely take the time to look back on some amazing moments and positive influences.

A large part of our lives is just a series of images. They pass us by like towns on a highway, without you really stopping to look and truly appreciate those moments. I have been, and still am, guilty of doing this, rather frequently.

When I look back on when I represented my country in a sports event, or when I graduated from university, achieved my Masters degree, and my travels around the world, I realise that I never really appreciated how monumental those moments were. Through life, I have met several people along the way, people who have been impressed by the fact I competed in sports at such a high level. Some of these people may not have had the opportunity to leave the town they grew up in, so travelling the world is a huge thing to them. Something I myself would not appreciate in the same way as them. But it is something I should appreciate, and it is something to be proud of. A lot of people take certain privileges for granted and, as mentioned, don't appreciate it at the time. I was, and probably still am, one of these people.

Even now, when my family compliment me on gaining my Master's degree whilst simultaneously competing and embarking on a new, challenging job, I just accept their praises and don't think much of it. If they had been talking about someone else having achieved this, I would probably have been impressed and possibly jealous. It isn't until you really think about how much you have done and achieved that you start to appreciate it all. But is it wrong for anyone to want more? Is it wrong for me to want more … to think that I may have more to offer to the world perhaps? Does this mean I'm being ungrateful for what I have, or is this a means of continuing to strive and better myself?

There are so many ways to look at this.

There are several people in this world who accept and agree that they lead a good life. They're unlikely to complain about who they are, what they do and where they are heading. I have a good friend who is very close to me. Despite this, they have a very different perspective on life, striving for things that may or may not be attainable. They have a good family, a good group of friends, enjoyed school, but did not go on to gain further qualifications. However, they've enjoyed their life, and were exposed to the usual childhood, teenage and adult experiences. They now have a family, a basic job and a partner they love. I think it's fair to say that they are content with life. They say they would honestly not ask for more and are happy with what they have done, where they are and how they see themselves now, and in the future. Is this the image of contentment and satisfaction we all aim for? I know another individual who is totally different to my friend. This person has experienced life in so many different ways. They have travelled the world, met many people from different backgrounds, been immersed in many cultures, fallen in and out of love, experienced various careers in different industries, at varying levels of responsibility, and they have some great friends. However, life is not quite good enough and they still want more. They are striving for that something that may not be possible to achieve. Perhaps they are looking for something that may complete them. They have spoken about wanting to leave their mark on the world, doing something that makes them memorable, and impactful on the people of this world.

How many people in the world actually reach this self-imposed goal?

How many people can honestly say that they have achieved something that will be remembered, something that will become their legacy? Must we leave a legacy in this world? When we go, how will people remember us? How will we have made a mark or a difference in this world? Will our footstep stay forever, or will it be blown away as the past?

In reality, each of us are only a small grain of sand on a beach several miles long. But when our time on this earth ends, will we live on in any way. There are some individuals, a handful of the human race, of those seven billion people, who really do leave their mark through an invention, skill, or action. It isn't always that the mark left is a positive action or a good choice. People can leave a reputation for the pain they caused or the bad decisions they made. Yet, they are remembered, and will be for a while. They have done something that has changed individuals, groups or even the world in one way or another. They have influenced other people's thoughts and way of life, which may, in turn, impact on future generations. Although, I would like to believe that there is still some justice in this world, even in a world that is currently spinning, full of grey and compromise, and full of uncertainty. I would like to believe that, if someone choses to do wrong towards you when you make choices, that you will stand up to that person or punish their decision. You hope that someone will take a stand and fight back to demonstrate that good choices do matter.

Is it better to be remembered, if only for a short period, by friends and family for being the good person, the good friend, and the positive influence you were? The legacy you leave are the children you brought into this world. The children you raised in the best way possible, hoping they will enjoy life and continue the family, and perhaps even leave a mark of their own. You also leave the legacy of having influenced friends and families, in the decisions they've made, or the paths they have chosen to follow. Your influence may be as simple as having made them smile and laugh when they needed to. You have had an influence, and you will be remembered for that.

It makes you wonder whether you made a similar impact on other people's lives, people you met briefly. Were we part of someone's life when their dream came true, or were we there when their dreams died? Did we help someone make a decision that shaped their life and time? Did we persevere with some people, as though we were destined to be in that individual's life to make a meaningful impact?

Just think, you could be a big part of someone else's life and not even know it. It only takes a small moment, a laugh or a smile to make a significant difference in one's life. It is these small moments that we often don't realise or appreciate.

There are people in this world who strive for greatness, people who wish to leave this world and be remembered for something great they did, to be able to live on in people's minds and memories. Whether this applies to people you know or strangers, it's what a lot of people would strive for and love. Is it enough to have a career, raise a family and leave this world content in the knowledge that come 20, 50, or a 100 years from today, your name will be forgotten ... you'll be just a memory or a photograph?

Chapter 13

I think my personality falls in the minority. I would love to do something iconic and memorable, not for fame, status, or money, but for the recognition of having something associated with my name, something I can leave to this world that could help others. Perhaps I have already achieved this, or perhaps I will get the chance to do it. I will bet that, if I do succeed with this desire, I would not appreciate the immensity of it at the time. I am definitely one of the personalities I spoke about previously, where I work hard to get something, then when I get there, I don't really appreciate it before I move on to wanting to better and beat my own achievement. I say I want to do something memorable, but if I managed this, would my next aspiration be to go another step further, rather than sit back, enjoy and appreciate what I have accomplished?

There are similar, more everyday examples you can use to visualise my type of personality: you could be training and aim to do a ten mile run. You reach your ten mile goal, but you don't stand back and applaud yourself for running those ten miles. Instead you tell yourself that if you can run ten miles, you should be able to run another five miles. You're convinced that ten miles isn't far, but 15 miles would really make it a worthwhile workout. Something to be proud of.

More impactful examples to illustrate this concept could be that you've completed your A-levels and decided to study further and attain a university degree. You obtain a good degree and chose to go beyond this and do a Master's degree. Finally, after a lot of blood, sweat and tears, you pass this and immediately seek to triumph it with a PhD. I have been through this thought process, where you always want that little bit more. Again, I ask, is this not a case of not being satisfied with what you have? Is it a form of greed and lack of appreciation of what you have? Or is it simply your inbuilt personality trait of always wanting to strive for more? Some people have this trait and find their actions unavoidable.

When you look back on your life, certain moments stand out. Maybe it's the day you graduated from high school, your wedding day, or the day you found out you were going to become a parent. There are a handful of moments that you will remember for the rest of your life. It is these moments that you need to really cherish. You shouldn't take them for granted, nor simply move on from them. Appreciate them when they come along because these moments can be few and far between. There may come a time when they cease completely.

I'm still uncertain about whether this is a personality trait that is good to have, or not. It is great to strive for more and improve on yourself, but is that being greedy and disillusioned? Especially as it may not be the best move for you. Perhaps at some point I should acknowledge that I have reached my peak, my potential, and I should be satisfied, rather than trying to aim for more. You did all you could to reach your goal. Is it right to keep fighting for something that may not be for you?

A well known example of someone at who sits on the extreme end of this, someone who I look up to and admire, is James Cracknall, the well known Olympian.

He has endured some of the hardest races and physical tests that anyone could push themselves to do. He pushes himself to mental and physical extremes. On the completion of his monumental rowing across the Atlantic, he sought his next challenge, and formed his next goal. He is the kind of person who needs something more to aim for. He needs a target, something immense, something he knows will require the training time, and will push his mind and body to its limits. It is these types of goals and achievements that give you the adrenaline rush you need to try more, do more, achieve more, and perhaps even fill that something you feel is missing.

As my personality is similar to these achievement-seekers, I find it easier to relate to and understand them. I do find it hard to believe that some people are truly satisfied with what they have. The kind who do not think about the possibilities of having that extra something they could accomplish or manage, were they to push themselves a little harder or further.

In my opinion, a lot of these people convince themselves that they are satisfied in their current state. They are just not motivated or confident enough to reach out for something extra, something more fulfilling. These people often lack the belief of successful achievements.

To be able to believe in a dream, chase it and make it happen, you need to have confidence in yourself and your capabilities. Without this confidence and intrinsic self-belief, you will never reach your destination.

If an individual says that they cannot do something, just ask them why they feel that way. Why can't they do it? What is their reason for not being able to achieve something? Is it because they lack the financial means, the intelligence, or time? All of these factors are represent obstacles along the way, but they are barriers that you can overcome. The list of possibilities is endless. If one person in the world can achieve something, then why can't you and I do the same? What is so different between one person to another? Yes, ideally certain physical traits are needed: a basketball player needs to be tall, a jockey needs to be short, a sumo wrestler needs to be, let's say, large; but it boils down to someone's belief, their state of mind or their thought process. Success is possible if one is not scared of trying and failing.

William Murray, a Scottish writer, stated, "Until one is committed, there is hesitancy, the chance to draw back, always ineffectiveness. Concerning all acts of initiative and creation, there is one elementary truth that ignorance of which tells countless ideas and splendid plans: that the moment one definitely commits oneself, the Providence moves too. All sorts of things occur to help one that would never otherwise have occurred. A whole stream of events issues from the decision, raising in one's favour all manner of unforeseen incidents and meetings and material assistance, which no man could have dreamed would come his way. Whatever you can do, or dream you can do, begin it. Boldness had genius, power, and magic in it. Begin it now." William Murray is probably trying to say that you don't know what you are capable of until you try, until you believe and until you are bold enough to push yourself. There will always be bumps in the road, and reasons for not doing something, but until you try, you would never know whether you could have found that something that was missing, or reached that goal you knew existed, or found that dream that became a reality.

Perhaps one day, when I'm old and grey, I will suddenly have the realisation that I had everything I wanted, and I will have to eat my words. I will see that, despite all my thinking, pondering and searching, in reality there was nothing else to look for and nothing else to find. I may have to look back and admit I was wrong, but at this point my life, I can honestly say that I can't comprehend how someone could say they were truly happy and satisfied with their life when they still had so much of it to live, to learn, to explore and find out, about themselves and others.

Perhaps when you are old and grey, and you have lived your life, things will be different. Your life may have been a fast paced one where you visited places, met new people, and experienced new things. Or you may have led a slower paced lifestyle where you met your partner, raised a family and enjoyed those moments of relaxation and having little to do. Whatever life you lead, when you are coming to the end, there should be a time when you look back and feel good about your accomplishments. Although, when you have so much of your life to live, I cannot see how you can already be fulfilled with it all and not want for more. When you are 80 or 90-years-old, you really can look back and, hopefully, be truly satisfied. So maybe you need to stop worrying about missing pieces of the puzzle right now and just live your life and enjoy the ride.

Is this a good way to be? Is it worth constantly improving

yourself and striving for more?

I am obviously biased in the way I describe things here as I am, as we have already established, one of those people who wants more. Perhaps if someone else, who is my age, has already started a family and is raising children with the love of their life, wrote this story, it would be written completely different. Being aware of this, I am trying my best to see it from both perspectives. After I've contemplated the other side, I may begin to better understand that alternative way of thinking and living.

I am not sure, and I don't think I will ever be sure, where these thoughts or feelings of constantly wanting more comes from. Some people think that it is about being unfulfilled emotionally. Perhaps due to a lack of acknowledgement from parents or others you look up to throughout your childhood.

For me, that hasn't been the case. I had a great upbringing, with a great family, great friends, and great role models. Perhaps it has more to do with a lack of acknowledgement from yourself, rather than from others. There will always be people who think differently, who focus on how well they are performing, and sometimes, this can turn into arrogance. On the other hand, not actually noting your accomplishments can often be just as diminishing to someone and the people around them.

Chapter 14

Everyone has something to offer in life and it could be different in the most subtlest of ways. This could be subtlety manifested in a musician, an author, an Olympian, a good parent, a good friend, a good child, sister or brother. I suppose the key is acknowledging your strengths and how these influence your life. A lot of it has to do with whether you choose to acknowledge what you have in your life rather than focusing on what missing is to fill the void you may have, and just living your life, rather than searching for something more.

You could sit at home and think of everything else that you might want, and of the possible additions you could make that would complete you that little bit more. Unfortunately, the old saying of "the grass is always greener on the other side", often isn't true.

You can pick anyone out of a line up and, regardless of whether they are in education, have just started a family, are male or female, and of any age, you will find they are missing something. There are opportunities they wish they'd taken and decisions they wish they'd made differently. I don't think anyone is ever free of these thoughts. If you think you are alone in this thinking, trust me, you are not.

People are so good at focusing on the negatives and ignoring the positives. We look at how the glass is half full. You focus on what you could have done, what you could have been, rather what you have and who you are.

If I am sure of anything, it is that everyone in this world has something that they have accomplished, something they can be proud of. It's common for people to think that they haven't found this something yet, but the problem actually lies in not acknowledging it and complimenting it. It's obvious to us when someone else does this, but it's not so clear when it comes to ourselves. It is clearly how we are made to behave, but it is something that needs to change if we are ever going to aim for contentment in life and ourselves.

However much we want to, we cannot go through life contemplating about the things that we have missed out on. If we do, we will never get anywhere. It will be difficult to move forward, and that isn't a life.

Some of my 25-year-old friends tell me that they haven't done much in their adult lives. They believe they should have reached a different point, and maybe have more to show from their time so far. Some say that they don't have children, or they aren't in a serious relationship, or they do not own their own home, or have a high-flying career. In reality though, if one were to dig deeper into their lives, they'd find that these people have been some of those greatest friends that others could only wish for. They have travelled a little and met various people from different cultures, with great families who absolutely adore them. So when you think about it, life's not so bad for them really. People see the tangible aspects of life, but these are not the things that matter. What matters is being a great friend, a great mother, father, son or daughter; it is about the ability to put a smile on someone's face and make someone laugh when they need it the most, especially if they don't ask for any support.

It is sometimes easy to write about difficulties, sometimes it's easier to talk to a stranger, but it takes courage whichever way it is shared, something that is not always easy to do when you're on your own.

I am living proof of this. I can spend a lot of time putting down on paper my every thought and feeling. Although, I often remind my friends and family how much they have to be proud of and how important it is for them to take a stand and take note of this. Yet, unless someone tells you, that insight is not always apparent to yourself, and you continue to strive for that extra satisfaction in your life.

Perhaps the issue isn't something that will ever go away, no matter how much people try to convince you otherwise. However, this is not something I will ever stop recommending to my friends. There will be something in everyone that others could feel jealous about, and I think it's important that they are aware of this and, even more importantly, they acknowledge this attribute themselves.

Perhaps you think something is missing from your life, and you want to try and find out what that is. The only way to do this is to keep pushing yourself in all areas of your life, particularly school, sports, music or family, in the hope that you will stumble across that missing piece of the puzzle at some point. Having this as a purpose in life will present you with the opportunity to sit back and relax with a sense of fulfilment because you are where you really belong.

Not having a sense of direction to follow could result in you wasting valuable searching time. Unless you get lucky and find that something, there's really no point in you continuing with your search. Would it make more sense to continue living your life and wait for that something to find you instead? It could be fame, fortune, love, or children. People freely throw about the phrases, "What will be, will be" or "everything happens for a reason".

People who believe that everything happens for a reason are usually the ones who have either been through or are going through a break-up, a lost job, or the loss of something important to them. When something like this happens to us, we naturally turn to well-known lessons to somehow reduce the pain. We will look for something that gives us that bit of hope to keep going. And yes, it can work.

Perhaps you need to understand and accept that it is OK to let yourself be happy because you never know how fleeting that happiness may be. Take life and accept it for how and what it is. Try not to analyse it too much. Perhaps that is my problem.

I have come across many people, some of whom are my good friends, who tend to overthink actions, outcomes and thoughts a little too much. This process forms the beginning of self-doubt in relation to themselves and their talents. Some of the people I know are highly talented in sports, music or education, but they aren't quite secure enough to believe the talent they have is sufficient. Consequently, they question aspects of their life and look to others for encouragement, reassurance and support. And this is fine, some people need this, but these are the same people who need to learn to acknowledge their talent and feel content with it and where it takes them.

The common phrases and beliefs mentioned above are the ones I have become accustomed to throughout my life. They have helped me through certain predicaments, at times when I was disappointed or low. Being a perfectionist, I'm rarely content with what I have and always want more. So my parents spent a considerable amount of time drilling these sayings into me. Many people live by the saying that if you work hard, that missing something in your life will find you. This does, in a way, make some sense, and you would hope that it was true. Although, when you think about it in more depth, these sayings can be misunderstood and potentially misleading. This take us right back to the argument about whether life is fair, regardless of the hard work you put in. It makes one question how big a role luck plays in your life and future. For some people, these generic sayings of "everything happens for a reason" actually do hold value. Others hear of these sayings and wonder whether there is a specific path mapped out for us? Or is it our responsibility to look for the perfect life, rather than letting it find us?

I have seen people who are intelligent, hard working, friendly, and generous, being brought back down to earth with a bang when denied something for no apparent reason. If whatever is denied is something that is very important in one's life, it impacts how they are as a person and where they end up.

I had a great friend who was one of the loveliest and most trustworthy people you could ever meet. In short, she was amazing. The type of person who would always put others before herself, someone you could always turn to. She was happily married and had formed a great career path for herself. She'd married the love of her life, they were perfect together and completely in love. But there was one thing she really wanted but couldn't have. We all know she would make a great mum, just from they way she was with younger people, friends and other members of her family. She truly was quite generous. If we take the familiar saying and believe that everything happens for a reason, what was the reason behind this situation?

This person was lucky enough to pinpoint what was missing, but not lucky enough to accept that what she wanted was actually unachievable. Perhaps it's good that she was unaware of the futility behind pursuing this goal. But did this then make her search for something else to fill her void? Another perspective on this situation could be that, despite not having her utmost desire for children fulfilled, she was given the opportunity to direct her positive nature to her friends and family members, to a much greater extent. In my opinion, she has definitely done this. She was the friend you went to if you needed someone to talk to or were in trouble. She was the auntie that her nieces and nephews would turn to for advice, or just to moan about mum and dad. She is someone who, with her dedication to hard work, has definitely made a difference in their career and their profession. She has had the chance to progress and reach the stage where her actions, decisions and outcomes have had an impact for the better, and perhaps that was the plan. Not one to be impressed or swayed by status' or titles, she valued people for who they were, and will always treat them as they would treat her … as a friend.

This is just one example of a good friend who has had a hard knock in life. There are billions of other similar examples in the world, like soldiers who are injured or killed whilst fighting for their country. There are amazing people in this world, people who have showered the world with smiles and have been a positive influence and ray of light for many others. Some of these great people die before their time. How can something like this be part of a plan?

Some would say this is a sceptical view to have. Perhaps it is wrong to dwell on negativity. To reject a saying, one that some people live their life by, is very subjective. If everything does happen for a reason, and this is the case in my life, then maybe there is thought and reason behind my mad desire to constantly reach further.

If it isn't going to come to you, then you have to go and get it, right?

Chapter 15

Can we really have it all? This must be a question asked by everyone at some point in their life. When you have a career, can you also have a family, or when you have a family, can you also have that something just for you, and you alone: a good career that you love, a hobby you can immerse yourself in, or just that something that can help define you as an individual; rather than just being a wife, a mother, a father, or a colleague.

I think everyone does need something for themselves, something that defines them, something that makes you, well … you.

This could be a career and profession, it could be a sport or a hobby that just makes you smile. It could be a skill you have, an individuality, or perhaps just being a great parent to your beautiful child.

There are millions of ways to define someone. If a person's negative traits outweigh the positive traits, then the only person who can turn this negativity around is the individual themselves.

It isn't easy for you to view yourself from the perspective others do. However, in order to really change things in your life, you need to be able to spot your positive and negative traits. Sometimes you're heading down a path and it's just easier and smoother to continue as you are, and with what you are doing. You need those to reflect on at certain periods in your life, to keep you on the right track. One that is right for you, not because it's the easiest way.

The best times to reflect is when the wind, the water, and yourself, are all still. It will last minutes, maybe even seconds, but it is these moments of stillness that give you the perfect opportunity to reflect and think.

Everyone needs moments like this as we have all experienced a time when we lose sight of ourselves, where we are going and who we want to be. There may be moments where you are ashamed of yourself or the choices you have made. However, everything you are ashamed of, everything about you that you try to keep secret, everything you want to change about yourself, is what makes you who you are. That is our power as individuals. Deny this and you are nothing. Embrace this and you become more powerful than ever.

Of course, like anything else, it may be uncomfortable initially. You find yourself in a new world and a new way of thinking for a while. It will feel awkward when you're forced to come out your comfort zone, one you've lived with for the past 20, 30, 40 years perhaps, whilst simultaneously trying to focus on finding your feet, continuing to live life, and moving forwards. Fear should not dictate thoughts and feelings though. Adventure, exhilaration, hunger and excitement for life and change would be more instrumental in leading the way forward.

Nobody is saying you have to jump off cliffs, swim with sharks, or jump out of a plane to live life to the full, but you should always try and push yourself and live boldly, to really get the most out of yourself.

You should never settle for a mediocre life, for a comfortable, run-of-the-mill life. Although, if you still insist on settling down and continuing your life with someone or something that isn't your ideal, make sure you still have a hint of that passion and adventure squirrelled away. Keep it somewhere where you can draw upon it later to ensure you still have, and will always, the possibility of fulfilling your excitement or luxury.

You are different at every point in your life. Your wants will also vary by the experiences you're exposed to. Tomorrow will be different to today. You will feel different and you will desire something different, but you are still the same person with the same deep desires. It's not always possible to replicate certain adventures. Even if you went to the same places and met the same people, it wouldn't be the same. Your experience wouldn't be the same. For me, undertaking an adventure and doing something new is all about the experience, the learning, and the new memories. It's about meeting new people, learning to not only appreciate a different culture, but actually experiencing and enjoying it like a native, and following whatever impulses strike you.

If you have the right mindset, it doesn't matter where you end up or how much money you pay, it will be something you remember forever, and it will begin to satisfy your inner desires. Ignoring them may result in you stagnating in your current life. A little voice in your head may tell you that there should be more. Sometimes you aren't exactly sure what that entails, but spontaneity plays an integral part in satisfying those desires, allowing you to be you.

It is your choice to take these desires and wishes and follow them. It is only you who can choose to do it, nobody else. It may take longer for some people to realise this and do something about it, but that's OK.

You have the time to change no matter how old or young you are. It takes these moments to realise what is missing in life and what can guide you. Sometimes we get overly concerned with the complexities, and then lose sight of the simplicity of life and the enjoyment it can provide.

Change is like an epidemic; it works in a very unusual way. When someone introduces something, it spreads from one person to another very quickly, then fades out gracefully.

This is how change works. Even the smallest change can get something started, and little changes can make a huge difference. The general expectation is that daily changes happen slowly and steadily, with there being some obvious relationship between cause and effect. In the event of sudden, significant changes, the element of surprise is hard to deal with. Making a change could require a small amend, something that could be unnoticed by other, but it could make an immense difference to your life and others.

It is never too late to make a change.

Sometimes you cannot take the past and completely erase it, but there are things that you can do to overcome past events. There is a chance that doing so will remind you that what you do and how you do it matters.

You may have made bad choices in the past, but there are ways of moving forward and finding happiness.

Bad or right is not an absolute state, it's more of a relative term. Let's take a thief who stole cash to feed his family, or the kidnapper who took the child to protect them from a neglected life, or the bully who was abused as a child … Just because someone breaks the law, their actions are classed as being wrong, but it doesn't necessarily mean they have crossed the line from good to evil. This line does creep up on some people, and before they know it, they are on the other side. Even then, everyone has the chance to come back, recognise the reason behind their actions, and find themselves again.

It's funny how our past can frame us. Sometimes, the person we used to be doesn't let go. It places a hold on the person we have become. Past failures, disappointments, and even victories, take hold of us. They can haunt us like ghosts, visiting like old friends, no matter how far we try to distance ourselves from them. There are times you are in a position to make a choice where you can change things, effectively pushing these ghosts aside. It forms the beginning stages of finally finding that missing piece of the puzzle, which has been haunting you all along.

Although, this doesn't really answer the initial question ... can we have it all? Can we have complete and utter satisfaction, fulfilment and happiness in all aspects of our life?

With me being me, and with my way of thinking, I think you can. I have strived, and will continue to strive, for this throughout my life. I maintained my sporting interest to the best of my ability whilst furthering my education and carving out a career. I thought I'd be able to pursue this and make a real difference to people, to have an impact. I have a good relationship with my family and have stayed close to my good friends whilst making new ones along the way. Perhaps it is possible to have it all, well there's hope anyway, but whether this is enough is the question. Again, to reiterate that initial question, is there something missing? Or am I searching for too much perfection, something that isn't there, and may never be?

Hope is the combination of wishing and believing in all forces external to us. Most often, the outcome of what we hope for is driven by the actions of others and, somewhat, the faith we have. Hope is the light at the end of the tunnel. It gives us the courage and strength to press on when we are busy working towards reaching our goals and overcoming life's obstacles and challenges.

Hope is a desire for something. If you want that energy and passion for the rest of your life, then you need some level of hope. I would hope to never lose my own hopes, no matter how bad or low I may feel, nor how successful I become.

Chapter 16

I still have a massive part of my life to live, so perhaps I'm not the best person to be posing these questions. Others who are older, wiser and more experienced in life may already have answers to the questions I have been asking. They will have lived through many aspects. Perhaps they also had moments where they thought they could have it all, thinking this would bring true happiness, make them truly satisfied. Similarly, they would have lived through the knowledge that this is not always attainable. Perhaps they may know whether this something that I, and others, are looking for, is real and possible, or whether just a form of greed and is realistically unattainable … so far nobody has been able to answer these questions. This could indicate that nobody really knows the answer because people are so focussed on their own lives, unaware of how others feel, think and act.

From the outside it might seem as though some people have the perfect life: a great family, a career they love, lovely possessions, but what lies beneath these external factors may be different.

The prettiest woman could have a troubled heart. A highly favoured colleague may be struggling to find love or start a family. The richest person you know, who has the car, the house, the clothes and the superstar lifestyle, may be lonely. Sometimes those who seem to have it all, lack their true desires.

Is it fair to aim for it all? Is it fair on those around you, those ones closest to you or those who are unable to reach beyond their current means, or even to people who have worked harder and longer with nothing much to show for it? It probably isn't. However, this could be as simple as understanding that what I see as having it all and wanting more, could be quite different for the next person, and the person after them. The definition and opinion of satisfaction, completeness and happiness in life does vary from person to person. That is a major point that I have taken on board whilst undergoing the thought process behind writing this book.

What may satisfy one person might just be a starting point for others. Some people I know have families and love staying at home to look after the children and other family members. They do not want a career. Their aim is to ensure their families lead better and easier lives. Others chose to focus on building a career. One where they can make a difference to the world. They see this as their legacy. Different people with different hopes and desires contribute to this ever-changing world.

Some like the familiarity of their towns, houses, and jobs. Therefore, they are happy to stay put and live out their lives in that familiar, safe surrounding. Others want to move on, perhaps to a different town, or different country even. They may often change jobs to grow and learn new things, challenging themselves constantly.

You grow up in this town, city or village, with the same people and go to the same places. You spend most of your time there, but it's not until you've grown up that you really get to know the place for what it is. The perspective of the town is different when you are older. Seeing the town at two o'clock on a Saturday morning would be different to what you saw in your younger years. You no longer see the good looking boys, or the jealous girls. You drive the same streets you walked down while in high school. You speak the same way and eat the same food. But it's nice. It's nice to see your home town in a new way, a fresh way. You see others possibly making the same mistakes and living the same lessons, and your heart aches for some of the experiences they will have, and the future that lies ahead of them. This doesn't mean you don't face any hardships, of course there have been and will always be hardships, but you have your life and it's good. However, you can't always stay put and drift along. Everyone needs to challenge themselves in some way.

For me, the possibility of staying put, starting a family early and not having a career of my own is not an option. As mentioned previously, I need to do things for myself, to constantly aim to better myself. Yes, having a family and looking after them will, at some point in my life, be a high priority. When that time comes, I will absolutely love it, but I will never lose sight of the things that make me who I am.

Yes, people are different and have different perceptions of satisfaction and happiness, but surely the idea of maximising happiness is the same for all.

Happiness can come from many angles: the company of good friends, a lover, the feeling you get when you make someone else's dream come true, or in the promise of hope renewed.

Some people find happiness through their jobs, some through their achievements, and some find happiness through their family and those closest to them. These are the people who are the happiest when it is time to go home at the end of the day. Not because they are eager to leave work, or glad to have finished their shift at work and are able to change out of their uniforms and get to the comfort of their own home, but because this is the time for them to be reunited with their families. You see some who find happiness with their partner, from simply being in their company, from the closeness of being with this person. These are the people who, when you see them, when you see their smile and the sparkle in their eyes, give you hope that true love really does exist. You see it when they don't even realise it.

Having been asked this question, and having had this discussion with numerous friends, family members and colleagues, I've found that everyone's answer is different. The question is:

"Can you ever be 100 per cent happy?"

Now, if I haven't confused you so far with all my questions and attempts to answer them, then this is where things will definitely become confusing. Based on my own thoughts, ones I've shared with you so far, you would probably think I would say "no" to this question. However, this is where I have to distinguish between being happy and satisfied or just being content.

Happiness is not a destination. It is a state of mind, and isn't often permanent. It comes and goes. If more people considered this, then maybe they would find happiness more often.

Happiness can be achieved from having a job you enjoy, having the partner you love, or having children and a great family.

Using my own life as an example, I cannot sit back and say I am not happy, because I am. Everything I have in my life brings me happiness, and I would not change any of it for the world. These things put a smile on my face, and that I love. My family, spending time with my beautiful niece and nephew, spending time with my friends, to small things like a good workout in the gym, a good result in an exam, or even just hearing a great song for the first time, just adds that spring in my step. Often it is the smaller things that bring us the most happiness.

But am I content? That is the real question, and the answer, one I cannot ignore, seems to be no.

Content, by definition, is feeling happy and comfortable with what you have.

This is where the feeling of there being something missing comes about. If I am happy but not content, I appreciate the great life I have with great people and things, but I feel as though something is yet to come, something that I am yet to find.

I have spoken to many people about this and asked them the same question. Most come back with the safe, easy and obvious answer: that they are truly happy. Although, others do take the time to think it through and come back with the answer that you can't ever truly be happy and content if you are always searching and striving for more. This is where I believe they are missing that something like myself. An opportunity, a person, or an event, we don't know, but there is something missing.

It is often said that if you keep striving and searching for something, it's likely you will never find it, you will never be truly happy and you will never feel content. You will continue through life feeling this way, and being unable to change this.

This something missing could come in the form of anything in the world, from something monumental like children or the perfect partner, to something less significant, like an enjoyable hobby or a perfectly decorated house. Whatever it is, it is never set in stone that these desires will bring anyone further happiness. It may bring them completeness and contentment though, and that is where the difference lies.

But again, this is only my opinion and how I feel. Others may disagree. It's possible that some will see this as a greedy and selfish perspective, but I think it's just honesty; it's just being real.

Surely everyone has moments where they sit back and think that there must be more to life than this. This thought process doesn't overrule all the good things in your life, nor does it negate the amazing people in your life. It's just a form of wondering whether there could or should be more.

Maybe it's those who have never truly experienced happiness who believe that total happiness is unattainable. Perhaps it is those who do not strive for more, don't reach for the stars or aim for a goal. They just cruise through life accepting whatever comes their way, never wanting more. Maybe it is those who seek total satisfaction who think it is impossible.

Again, being the sort of person who searches for perfection, I believe you can achieve 100 per cent happiness.

However, this optimism stops at the idea of being 100 per cent complete and content. At this moment in time, I'm not sure whether this is possible.

I've tried to speak to people about this, partly as research for my writing, and partly because I'm intrigued to know whether other people I know, those I am close to and who have influenced me, feel similarly, or whether I am the outlier with these thoughts and feelings.

A friend, who I met in my early twenties, gave me an honest answer. When she was with her first husband, she thought she was happy. With two children, a good job, great friends, and no money worries, she had nothing to complain about and therefore assumed she was happy. She didn't know any different. This was her life, one she enjoyed, and she just assumed that happiness meant contentment.

It wasn't until she split up with her husband and found the man she was actually meant to be with, the person that truly made her happy, that she realised she was closer to being content. It's fairly safe to say that you don't know how far from true contentment you are as no one has full clarity about what they need. You could be living life thinking that things couldn't get any better, but when you take a step back and view your life and everything around you, you may find there is something out there that can push you forward towards contentment. Some people, on the other hand, do know what they are looking for and are more aware of it when they find it ... if they find it.

Again, based on the conversations I've had with different people, seeking different perspectives, I've come across people who do know deep down what it is they want and what they need to gain this. However, I found that these people can also be resistant, thinking they need to travel the world and experience everything they can before they reach contentment. Actually, they could just as easily be satisfied with a decent career, a loving partner and a family. A traditional family and life would let you relax and enjoy life. It's sometimes what people need. By being resistant to this idea, people spend years looking for that special or extraordinary fragment, thinking it forms the missing piece of the puzzle that would ensure their lives met expectations. People travel around, take part in random activities and tasks, but even having travelled across different countries, tasted different jobs, and different locations, they often return to the idea that a traditional family life would make them happy and, perhaps, content even. So you're not the inventor of a miracle cure, you're not a famous artist making an impression on the world, but you could, and probably would, be happy. That is the first step to contentment, surely.

It can take a while to get there, but when people realise what they want and how lucky they are to have finally got to that point of knowing what they want, they are a lot closer to contentment. Yes, finding that right person and starting a family doesn't just happen overnight. It isn't a simple case of stepping out onto the street and picking the first person who happens to be walking past. To know what you want is a huge asset, something that shouldn't be disregarded.

My own thoughts on happiness and satisfaction have followed this line of thinking. When you are in this mindset, it is really hard to view it from another perspective as it becomes engrained in your personality, and is sometimes irreversible. To some extent, the only way to gain a different perspective is by looking at the lives friends and families lead.

I had a special male friend in my life for a while, a close friend and a good guy.

I asked him the same questions in a general conversation: was he was happy and whether he thought someone could be 100 per cent happy?

He had a job he absolutely loved, one that suited him perfectly, a close family, a wife, children who adored him and activities that kept him fit and healthy, yet he said that he had never been totally happy. He didn't think that could ever happen or that anyone really was happy to that extent. He was of the mindset that, despite having all the amazing things in his life, he could never say that anything in his life made him feel perfect, and therefore 100 per cent happy. So what else could help him achieve this status. Perhaps he was actually in the wrong job, destined for more, destined for greatness, but didn't have the time, or hadn't taken the time, to find the means that would lead him to this greatness. Perhaps he was with the wrong person, but circumstances had worked in a way that meant that this was the path he had chosen.

Maybe he was living a life where it seemed like he was doing the right things, which is very different to living a life where you are actually doing what's right for you.

You could be agreeing to things that suit others better and denying yourself opportunities. This does happen when you have family and close friends around you. Sometimes, and actually most of the time, you have to put other people's needs first. This is absolutely the right thing to do, and the way you should be, but sometimes this results in you forgoing opportunities to better yourself and, in the course of this, finding that something missing in your life. I suppose this is something that happens to everyone. You have to accept it gracefully and live with it.

These influence your decision making and the choices you make. It is especially important if your life is about meeting the expectations and standards of the social and family culture you're exposed to. A lot of people go through life trying to conform to these ideologies, ones that were created along the way. Sometime it is easy to get caught in a life that seems right to others, but it's not what you really wanted from life, ultimately making you unhappy. By the time you realise this isn't the life that fulfils you, you are stuck with this life you have formed for yourself, but it is not your own.

There are certain sayings that are applicable to a lot of circumstances, such as, "I'm looking, but I don't know what I'm looking for. Maybe everything, maybe nothing, but I'll know when I find it."

I think a lot of people find themselves in this situation, where timing and circumstances hold you back from finding that something missing.

You are propelled into circumstances and situations that lead on to a life that may not be your own or of your choosing, but it is a path that you have no choice but to follow.

Although, could it be a matter of being propelled into this life for a reason bigger than just you? It could also be that you've found the missing piece of the puzzle because, as the saying goes, you aren't sure what you are looking for, so perhaps that's the reason.

Homes, cars, money, clothes, food, gym, opportunities, movies, games, events, church, friends, choices, work, family, spouse, kids, being plugged in … for some, this may not be enough.

We've all been there, surely. We've spent our adult lives looking for that one last puzzle piece ¾ be it financial success, the perfect relationship, owning a home in a nice neighbourhood, whatever ¾ and we are shocked when we find out that none of the pieces actually fit. So we try to manipulate them, forcing them into the vacant spaces of our lives, but somehow it doesn't always work.

Chapter 17

So what do you do next?

Do you give up and accept that this is it? Perhaps this is where you were supposed to be at this point in your life. Or perhaps you continue down the road thinking you will come across "it" at some point if you look hard and long enough.

Different people choose different routes. My male friend, the one I referred to earlier, chose to accept the good life he had. It may not be perfect to him and it's not where he saw himself, but he was living it. Although there may be other things waiting for him out there, he believed his time would be better spent making the life he had as good as it could possibly be, pushing aside those other thoughts and feelings, hoping they would go away.

Some believe that if you are content with life but still feel that something is missing, then no matter how much you try and cover it up with work, family or activities, however busy you keep yourself, this feeling is unlikely to go away. You would probably end up living with it. So is it better to live life suppressing these feeling or would you rather live out your life knowing you have done all you can to look for and find that final piece of the puzzle where you can have the opportunity to love your life and be 100 per cent happy and content.

Maybe it is just about timing.

If I would have left work ten minutes earlier, I may have bumped into the love of my life in the supermarket on the way home, perhaps we'd both be reaching for the same pint of milk. If I had reacted a second earlier, I may not have injured my knee and I'd still be able to pursue my sport and reach the heights that I can only dream of now. Or if I'd have done that extra hour of studying, I might have known the answer to the question in the exam, all I would have needed to achieve that higher grade, and perhaps the job of my dreams.

For some time, an event has been taking shape, one of those destinies of place and circumstance. Something we'd all be unaware of. If someone spent an extra two minutes in the shower in the morning, if someone had waited for their dog to retrieve the stick they threw, instead of walking home, or if you had sat down to eat your breakfast, rather than grabbing a piece of toast on the way out, your day may have been different, perhaps even life-changing.

Each of these things are just minor tweaks to your normal routine, but could these small events have changed the fabric of what would be for you?

An event or action is always taking shape somewhere, it's all about circumstance and place. You are unaware of it, the people around you are unaware of it, but it is happening and sometimes you have no control over it, the stage is set.

You gain confidence, courage and strength through every experience in life.

However, it is the ones where you really stop to look fear in the face that we take note of. You should be able to say to yourself, "I have lived through this and I have learnt from this". It sets you up to take on the next hurdle that comes your way, because you have learnt.

Sometimes you say or do things to cover up for some issues that you just don't know how to talk about or deal with. It shows that, perhaps, who we are isn't so much about what we do, but more about the decisions we make and our capabilities when we least expect it. It is about not being scared and not letting fear take you away from places or choices that you would usually make.

Every situation I have been in so far has changed me as a person. Sometimes you are not aware of the lesson you have learnt, or the changes you have made, but they do happen and they affect your future decisions and actions, sometimes without you even noticing.

There must be something pushing us to make certain choices, to take specific actions at specific times. Is there something directing us towards the destination that has been paved out for us, something that we really do not have a say in? If we are not content then, however hard we search, whatever journey we embark on, we will end up at the destination that has been decided for us, with people who have been chosen for us.

If you feel that whatever you do, or whatever you try, is irrelevant as you feel that no matter how hard you work, your road is already paved out. This will surely create a kind of disconnect.

When you're disconnected from your true self, you will feel as though something is missing because something is missing … YOU! It's the passion that naturally comes with being your genuine self, from being the real you.

Surely this isn't a good way to think or a good state of mind to be in. If fate exists, then it is fated that we create our own lives and draw our own paths. From what I have experienced, seen and understood, there are influences that you cannot change. These will certainly affect your life and those around you, but it is up to you to make the most of these and turn them into something you can live with, something that you can be excited about.

Everyone goes through moments where they think the world is against them and that everything is going wrong. You may think that you are alone in feeling like this and you're the only one who has to deal with it all. In reality, there are thousands, even millions of people facing similar issues and troubles every day.

You can choose to blame your circumstances on fate, bad luck or bad choice. Or you can fight back. You can take responsibility and accountability for your own decisions and your own life choices, and understand that it isn't just you who's experiencing this. Others go through similar devastations, heart breaks, and disappointments.

Sometimes people let pain become such a huge part of their life, they expect it to always be there as they can't remember a time when it wasn't.

One day, though, you may feel something else, something that feels wrong because it is so foreign and unfamiliar.

This can be the moment that you realise you aren't in pain, but actually happy. The rest of your life is being shaped right now, with every choice you make and every turn you take. You are being shaped by the choices you make and the person you choose to be.

You have the rest of your life to live, but it starts right now, with every tiny step you take, with every minute of the day, whether you want it to or not.

Henry James, an American writer, once wrote, "*Be not afraid of life. Believe that life is worth living, and your belief will help you create the fact.*"

In his writing, Henry James encourages the positive exuberance needed to live the best life you can. He also encourages people to not be afraid of taking risks, but take these willingly. If things go wrong, you learn from mistakes made, but it is best not to stand back and wait as life passes you by. You live it as hard and as full as possible.

I hope that this is what I have chosen to do. I hope that if I was to look back at my life, in 50 or 60 years time, I would see that I hadn't been afraid and that I tried.

OK, I may have a few failures under my belt, but that's all part of life, right?

Obviously there are things I regret, things I would like to take back, things I would change if I could, but we all have to live with the residue of our choices, and the consequence of our actions. When looking back, you will remember some occasions that you wish you could have changed, tears you wish you had never shed, times that you could have better spent, and frustrations you should have shrugged off. Life can be full of regrets and it's normal to wish you could turn back the clock to live parts of your life over again. Throughout my life so far, I have loved, I have lied, I have hurt, I have lost, I have missed, I have trusted and I have made mistakes, but most of all, I have experienced and learnt. Surely that is all anyone wants.

Sometimes it's hard to see how you got to where you are. Often when you look back, it is not obvious what occurred and why, who you are and who you will become. However, if you've lived up to the positive reasoning's of taking risks and living life, it is likely that you will end up where you are supposed to be. I believe that the sense of possibility we need for happiness, success and a life of minimal regrets comes from within us, and from our parents. Other factors that could influence this sense include the stage we are at in life and any opportunities we have been presented with in the past.

Chapter 18

As much as we try to fight it, our parents have some kind of mystical hold over us for a large part our lives. It instils our way of thinking, influences the choices we make and the paths we tend to follow. They have the potential to affect our emotions and thoughts in a way only parents could do.

Life can be hard. There are difficult choices to make, some that could have disastrous consequences. Children need guidance, I definitely did and often still do. This guidance influenced the good decisions I made and also helped me avoid many mistakes. Parents lead by mouth, and by example. If a child's idol or hero is one or both of their parents, then the road of experience and learning becomes smoother. Every bit of this smoothing helps us cope with the rough world children are faced with when they become adults, even at the earliest point. A point in their lives where they are devoid of magic and charm, and the beauty of innocence and imagination.

The relationship between a child and their parent is a bond that changes over time, but it never diminishes, regardless of whether they are in the same room, a nearby town, or even half a world away. They could be in another world entirely and the bond would still be strong. It's a power we have never fully understood, one I don't think we ever will, or ever should. However, we can be safe in the knowledge that the bond is there and it is one of the strongest bonds you will ever have and feel.

Family form a huge part of everyone's life, whether you like it or not. They may influence you negatively or positively, there will be instances of happy experiences or frustrating ones, but you are stuck with the family you are given. Other things may change, but we start and end with the same family in our lives.

We all know you can't choose who your family are, but you can influence how it will be and how you interact with one another. You can control whether you have the family you only see or talk to at Christmas, the kind you send the odd birthday card to, or you can be the kind of family who are friends, who are there for one another now and forever. I am fortunate to be part of a family who I love, the kind of family that would make an effort to stay in touch, understand one another, and see regularly.

Unfortunately, there are a lot of people who deliberately appear too busy to notice that they are missing out on precious time with family, the only people who you are supposed to know the best and be able to trust with your life. You don't want to miss the opportunity to form memories. Surely you would want to grab any opportunity to spend time with family, enjoy the moment, and create those memories.

Family is often taken for granted. Actually, family is taken for granted throughout life. This is obvious when, in rare moments, things are said or done to suggest that family were taken for granted. It could be when you are away from home for the first time, at university perhaps, and you become ill and just want a cuddle and for someone to look after you. Or when you have just moved out and have had a horrible day at work and just need someone to moan to. Or that time when you're feeling a little insecure after a break-up and just want your family around. Each person realises this at different times in their lives, and for different reasons.

I would like to say that I have always known how lucky I am to have the parents I have been blessed with, but I don't think that's true. Like all children and teenagers, I took them for granted. I expected to be driven around the country for sport, to see friends or family. I expected nice holidays, fun weekends, the birthdays and the Christmas presents I wanted. I think it's true that the more you get, the more you expect. Although, this is a common theme across most children. It isn't until you reach an age where you start to fend for yourself, undertaking small tasks, from the day-to-day chores of washing, cleaning and cooking, to managing your budget so you can afford a weekend away with friends or more extravagant holidays. Of course, by the time you realise it, it is often too late to say thank you. You hope that your parents are aware, I would really hope mine are. Not everyone is blessed with the kind of family I grew up with, but every individual would have learnt something from their parents. This may be what to do, how to act, what to say, or who not to be. But, like all things in life, your parents will influence you and help shape you into who you are today, more than anything else.

Luckily, I am, and have always been really close to my family. Not just with close family as in my mum, my dad and my brother, but also with my grandparents, aunties, uncles and cousins. I'm not saying this is down to me, because it isn't. It is an extension of the tight knit family relations my grandparents and parents have. One that was ready and waiting for me.

My parents began this by ensuring that my brother and I had a close relationship. With only a couple of years between us, which helped. Our parents ensured we had interests in common and that we learnt to get on together and look after one another.

Of course we argued and fought about stupid things, like who would get to sit in the front seat of the car or who got to watch their programmes on the television, but when I think about it, our amazing memories outweigh the arguments and fights by a long way.

Sport was always something that brought out the best and worst in both my brother and myself. We were both sporty, which meant we were both competitive. This often meant an argument would be brewing. We would compete in any sport, from badminton to tennis, from swimming to something like ten pin bowling. We were always in competition, but never in a nasty way. Just a healthy competitive way, with both of us having the will to win and the confidence in ourselves. This healthy competition only pushed me further and played a larger part in my life than I really knew at the time. Having that competitive streak and the mindset to constantly push myself from an early age only helped me with my future sporting lifestyle and my continuous desire to grow and develop, not just in sport but in my career and general life as well. I hope I had the same effect on my brother, the way he did on me when we were younger. Even if I only affected him with five per cent of what he did for me, I would be pleased.

On weekends, it used to surprise my friends when I said I was going somewhere with my brother. A few of them thought it was odd that I could spend time with him alone or when he was with his friends, and have a great time. I, on the other hand, find it strange that others couldn't do the same. Surely you feel the most comfortable around your parents and siblings. People you can relax around and just be yourself and never have to change for. Well, that's how I have always felt with my brother. When I joined my brother for a night out with his friends, I always felt included, accepted and wanted. That was due to our close relationship and our similarities.

My brother didn't follow a similar path through life. He formed his own path, which has not only suited him as a person, but has made my life even better. My brother gave me an amazing nephew and a beautiful niece. He has shown me how someone can just turn from being my older brother into an amazing dad, and a complete and amazing person. He has shown me how being a parent can come naturally to some. Despite having a family of his own, he is still there for me whenever I need him. Although he has not experienced what I have, with a different set of ups and downs, he has grown up in the most positives of ways. I can only hope that I can be grounded in the same way he has been throughout my life. Quite a lot of people say that they have the best family in the world, but perhaps we could rephrase this. I have the best family I could ever ask for. They enhance my life, give me hope, show me love and push me forward. What more could you really ask for from a group of people that you have to spend your life with.

My family is a collective expression of individual perspectives, a living work of art created over time, from one generation to the next. Opinions, expressions and beliefs are passed on, revisited and often revised, but they form the basis of this work of art of that I have become a part of and would not ever change.

Have you ever looked at yourself in the mirror and wondered who it is staring back at you?

Is it the person you want to be, the person you dreamed you'd be, the person you know you can be, or is there someone else you were supposed to be and you've fallen short?

Whichever one of these apply, it is often down to the influence of your friends and most of all your family.

Does someone stare back at you and tell you that you can't or you won't, when anything is possible when you really put your mind to it?

It is up to you to believe that dreams come true, and that love and happiness is out there waiting for you. Only you can make this belief become reality. Money, fame or power don't necessary bring love, but it can come from good friends, family and from the quiet nobility of leading a good long life.

You need to believe that dreams come true, because they do.

Next time you look in the mirror, remind yourself of what you've learnt from your family and others. Remind yourself that you can be happy, and you deserve to be.

Chapter 19

Perhaps timing plays a larger role when it comes to that missing piece of the puzzle. Although, timing isn't something that we can really affect: we left at that specific time for a reason; we stopped at that point for a particular purpose.

Is it possible that this has more to do with the fact that people settle for something that may not be right for them at that particular moment. Perhaps people use timing as an excuse to mask their fear or regrets. It is something that is beyond their control, so it could be an easy target for blame, when in reality they only have themselves to blame.

You could meet someone and be with them for years, but that doesn't necessarily mean this person is right for you. Is this person your perfect partner, or was this union more a matter of convenience?

Many people have relationships, some that last for a number of years, and generally seem happy together. However, some of these people end up in the arms of someone else, without really understanding why. How is it possible for a person to vow to be with someone forever, then venture towards another, especially when they've paved a life with the partner they vowed to be with? But if you look at things closely sometimes, although I can't believe I'm saying this, you can sometimes see how this happens and the path it follows. The majority of these situations arise because people are weak. They think the grass is greener elsewhere and believe they can do better than what or who they have. It could be a case of someone realising they are with someone who does not complete them, someone they settled with in order to lead a comfortable life, but clearly not the right life. In a twist of fate, this person may have stumbled upon someone they weren't seeking, but who turned out to be the one for them. This is often obvious to the both of them. On finding this person, they realise that they have found the missing piece of the puzzle, that this is the person they need to be with to be content in their life.

Should this person ignore that connection and that bond because of the circumstances? They were already with someone, and had possibly settled down, but is this a reason to ignore the opportunity for completeness and contentment? Or should they give in, realising that they only have one life, and choose to live it with as much happiness and contentment as possible?

Something can be missing even if people have been in the same relationship for years, despite being suitably matched and generally happy. Many people cannot tell you what is missing, but something is off. You can look at a relationship as a living entity. If you're missing a mere one per cent of a fingernail or a hair on your head, then it wouldn't matter too much. But if it is the heart that is missing, then this is a different matter. The entity would not survive, so maybe the relationship won't either.

Hearts are broken in the process and, in situations as these, feelings are hurt and people fall out. Although, at the end of the day, these people have the opportunity to find true happiness. This may not just positively affect the person who has managed to find that special someone. Perhaps this presents the opportunity for the other person in the relationship to find their something missing too.

This something missing may not be a person or a relationship. It may be a new career, a new home, or a new hobby, but it will be something that affects their life for the better, bringing them one step closer to feeling content.

Life has infinite possibilities. It is up to you to take each one as it comes and make the most of them. It is also our responsibility to seek out these possibilities and experience as many as possible. It is my opinion that, if one person in a relationship doesn't think that the two of you are really meant to be together, then deep down the other person knows it too. It may be harder for one to accept this, but in time, they will. Deep down they know that there is something more in life to be found, whether they admit it or not.

Right or wrong, I don't know, but I think that it is often a view and opinion that is lost in the argument, that cheating on your partner is wrong. However, it is something that needs to be acknowledged.

If you had the chance to be happy, and I don't mean just satisfied, but truly happy and content with everything you had, would you take it?

Just something to think about perhaps and just an opinion for a widely discussed topic, I'm sure.

Chapter 20

So what happens when you think you've found that something, perhaps that someone who completes you? This person totally and utterly gets you and everything about you. They make you feel special for your qualities, your faults and your flaws. You can be yourself around them and they never question you.

Everyone wants the kind of love that completely consumes them. They want that passion, adventure, and perhaps the element of a little fear, that completely fills them.

Every one of us hopes that we can find that someone who kindles the love in our heart. We want that ordinary person who becomes extraordinary to you.

You think you are in love and that this is it, that if you were to live your life with this person for the rest of your life you would be happy. When they kiss or hold you, your whole universe snaps back into place. It is possible to find that one person, and hope that they step up to the mark of being the person you can love, cherish and rely on. Every once in a while, people do step up and rise above themselves to meet you with your feelings. Sometimes they surprise you, sometimes they fall short and disappoint you, but this is normal in relationships.

Life is funny sometimes. It can push pretty hard, but if you look close enough, you will find that something, or that someone, and see hope in the eyes of the person you love. If you're lucky, perhaps one of the luckiest people on earth, the person you love will love you back. They will be your friend and soul mate. The feeling you get when holding the hand of someone you truly love is one that is hard to describe. I'm not referring to a passing attempt at holding hands, forming a loose link between you. I mean the kind of hand holding where your fingers map each other's knuckles and nails, the pulses in your wrists beat together as one, forming a strong connection between you. Even people who have been together for 50 or 60 years find it difficult to explain, or even understand why they love each other, and the feeling they get when together. Often it is not for the reasons we would first assume. Someone will swim into the space in your heart, and trying to understand why they are there is often hard to explain. Love is not an equation, it does not have a simple answer. It is more like a contract, the foundation of buildings, or the slate under chalk. It is having someone take care of you when you're unable to take care of yourself, and it is the place you return to, no matter where you were heading.

However we look at love, it is a force of nature. We may want to and may even try to control, command, demand or deny it. We have as much control over this as we do over the moon and the stars.

Love is bigger than ourselves. You can invite love in, but you cannot choose where it comes from or when. It strikes like lightening, and is irrefutable and unpredictable.

It doesn't come with its own set of rules, stipulations or conditions. You cannot make someone love you, nor can you stop yourself loving someone. It's not something that can be turned on and off. Infatuation can be used as bait. It can be switched on and off and imitated. But true love can never be replicated, nor can it ever be explained. When you fall in love, the other person has the ability to affect you in many ways. They can change your perspective on life, encourage you to make something of yourself, to travel places, or have ambitions. They can change the way you think and view things, and even influence how you think about yourself. The effect is so powerful, you may feel like you've lived more in the first six months or year of the relationship than you did in the last 20 or 30 years of your life.

You become absorbed with the person you love. It may be someone you wouldn't have met under normal circumstances, or someone you nearly missed. Perhaps you didn't like this person at first, but once you got to know them, you understood each other perfectly. You have adventures together, go places you may never have considered going to or you do things you would never have imagined. This person creates a world of wonder and possibility for you. A world full of electric skies and iridescent seas, a life of jokes, laughter and smiles. Time slows down and you appreciate that life is better with this person in it. Someone can be etched onto your heart, changing your life in a short amount of time, but remain there forever.

You know you're in love when everything you do brings you back to that special someone. You wake up and that person is the first thing that enters your mind. You count the minutes until you next see or speak to them. Just thinking about them makes you smile. Their errors and mistakes still make you laugh and all you want to do is be with them.

The fights and disagreements have no impact on your love for them. They are your best friend and soul mate, and your lover.

A soul mate, just two little words, but one big concept. A belief that someone holds the key to your heart and your dreams. The only thing you have to do is find them, your other half. Do soul mates actually exist, or is this just a form of torture for the many lonely hearts out there? Is this something we have just been led to believe in and search for … that person you will inevitably spend the rest of your life with, the ying to your yang? Does it always have to be your partner or a lover, or can your soul mate be a family member or a close friend? Can it be someone who you are comfortable with, someone you fit and connect with … someone who isn't your husband or wife but the person who gets you and understands.

Soul mates are described as "a twin soul, a person whom one has deep affinity, similarity and compatibility with".

Does that mean people still search for this perfect partner when they already have their soul mate in their life, just in a different form to what they were expecting? Most people are looking for their future husband or wife, someone they can build a family and life with, but surely we have to be ready and open to the fact that perhaps not all of us will meet this special someone. It is very likely that, when you find your soul mate, you'll know it. Although, I don't think every person in the world will find their soul mate in the form of someone they can spend forever with. Perhaps because of this, the idea of a soul mate is just another way of torturing ourselves. Are we pushing ourselves to find that special someone who will form the missing piece of the puzzle, that missing something in our lives that will be there forever?

In the course of searching, whilst we are focused on what we need to find, or what we believe we need to find, we are letting other great parts of our lives move rapidly past us. Things that could help us continue down our paths, one of which may be the path to feeling complete. Could the idea of a soul mate be a distraction from the rest of our lives, one that could be wonderful and fulfilling?

So where is this person? If you loved someone and it didn't work out, does this mean that this individual was never really your soul mate? Were they just a runner up in this game show called happily ever after? As you move through life, and the contestants become fewer and fewer, does that mean you have less of a chance of finding that special someone and getting your own happily ever after?

I think this is the point where people end up settling for something they believe to be love, their missing piece of the puzzle. In my life, I have witnessed friends and family settle down. However, some people settle for the sake of settling down. In a life full of high expectations, people get to the point where they wonder whether it is time to settle for what you can get. In my case, I refuse to settle for anything other than butterflies. I don't want to be with someone I think I should be with. I want to be with the person I need to be with, even if it takes me 10, 20 or 30 years to find that person, then so be it. I'm confident that I will know when I find them. Either way, I'm in no rush.

Chapter 21

I guess it comes back to that age old question of whether there is that one person in the world you are meant to be with. That one person who can complete you … the person you are supposed to spend the rest of your life with. I think the people who believe in a soul mate are those few who were lucky enough to have found the love of their life and lucky enough for everything to have worked out for them. They meet their partner, have fun for a while, get a little more serious, maybe move in together, get married, have children and live happily ever after. Or maybe they experience a different set of events together, but create their own happily ever after. The majority of people, on the other hand, hold the opposite view; a view that I share. These people believe that there are several people out there that you could be compatible with and fall in love with. You may become instantly attracted to a person, others you may fall in love with over time, and there may be some who you learn to love. With billions of people in the world, I don't accept that there is only one right person for each of us.

What happens if we meet this right person, this person who

is supposed to be our one great love, and then things don't work out? It's possible that we may mess things up and push them away. Does this mean we've come to the end of our search? Do we give up and accept that this is it, that there will always be that missing piece that you will never find?

It's scary to think that if you lose the one person you are supposed to be with, there won't be a second person waiting for you in the wings, just around the corner. If you don't have the belief and hope of finding someone to share the rest of your life with, then I'm not certain how one can go about life believing they can be happy in life on their own, without someone to share it with. It is the hope of finding someone that keeps a lot of people going. The hope that you are not alone, and that whilst you are looking, or even waiting for that person to find you, you have your friends and family, and your careers and hobbies to keep you going.

Hope is an amazing thing. It builds your day, it propels you forward, and helps you believe that you, and all of those around you, can have what you wish for.

We all have to be open to the fact that there are people out there who are better suited to others, and we have to keep hoping that our day will come.

It is possible that you will find someone you have an instant connection and chemistry with, someone you cannot ignore or deny, if you continue to have that hope. There are people you are drawn to, who are also drawn to you. If you're lucky, you will find each other. But if it doesn't work out, there's no need to fear that you are doomed forever. You do have the chance to brush yourself off and try again. Keep searching for that person who will make you happy and fill that gap. Hope will help you find it, and when you do, you will know it.

If you keep searching for that happy ending, pushing and pushing to find something that may not be ready for you yet, you are never going to find it, never going to get it right. However, if you sit back and enjoy the life you have, it will happen and you will get your happily ever after.

It is also a possibility that you may meet someone you connect with, but something may go wrong. Something that may not be within your control or their control. Some things just don't work out and sometimes we don't understand why.

You can spend weeks, months, or years getting to know someone, learning everything about them and eventually falling in love with them. You are soul mates and you believe that nothing will ever change that, but things do change, people change, people leave.

Surely something that completes you is permanent, but how permanent can a relationship be. OK, maybe I'm a cynic, because in my 25 years I haven't found someone who could become a permanent fixture in my life. Although, I have come across people who I thought could and would become a permanent fixture. I have experienced that feeling of love where you think that life couldn't get any better if you were to live out the rest of your days with just this one person. Despite this, I am still not convinced that that person was my soul mate, the person I was meant to be with. Things didn't work out, but my hope keeps me going.

A lot of people, myself included, have that nagging doubt, that what if, about the possibility of everything changing.

What if I gave someone my heart and things didn't go in the way I expected, with the relationship not working out? What if they broke my heart?

What if I placed all my hopes and dreams into one person and they stomped all over it?

What if we took steps forward but weren't actually meant to be together? What if there was someone else better suited for me?

Is it normal for someone to be thinking like this? I'm not so sure.

When it comes to relationships, would it be smarter to follow your head rather than your heart? There are hugely conflicting views about this. Generally, in life, not just relationships, I have always followed my head and ignored my heart. Perhaps, in the process of being quite driven and determined to make my mark in the world, and the fact I'm not afraid of being on my own, or feel the need to be in a relationship, I have ignored any feelings in my heart and followed my head. I followed what I thought I should be doing, rather than what I should have given into perhaps. There is a chance I may have missed out on potential relationships, opportunities and feelings in doing this, but I will never know. All these feelings, doubts and confusion probably go out the window when you find that Mr Right (or Mrs Right). Yet, I have friends who are getting married and having children, who still wonder whether they will ever end up with that certain someone.

So maybe these thoughts prevail even when you are in love, but something bigger takes over you, your heart, and your head, and those thoughts quieten down.

Does this mean that perfect partner is what was missing? Would finding your soul mate, or being with the person you think you should be with, solve everything?

Can a relationship have that effect on a person? Can it bring someone back to life? Can it put that spring back in your step and light that fire inside you? Can a relationship, or just one person, really do that?

When you are down, could someone be there to lift your spirits? If you have good news is there someone that you would want to share that with? When all your dreams come true, who do you want standing next to you to share those moments?

Sometimes a particular moment can leave us stunned momentarily when it happens. We know that this instant is more than a fleeting image. We know that this moment, every part of it, will live on forever. If you could, would you want to spend that moment with someone, would this someone make this moment seem more complete?

There is a chance that you will find the perfect person who fills that void the whole time you are together. Everything seems pleasing and you couldn't wish for anything more. Every moment you are with them, your heart beats faster and time speeds up. When you are away from them, all you want to do is be with them. You stare at your phone waiting for their name to appear as a phone call. Even a short text message puts a smile on your face. They are the first thing you think of when you wake up and the last thing you think of when you go to sleep at night. Perhaps, before you met this person, you thought you had everything you needed to make you happy. You had nothing else to compare it to, and it didn't seem as though you were missing something. Then this person walks into your life and everything changes. Your life has a different outlook, a different perspective and feeling. You realise how empty your world was without this person, and you suddenly see that your old life would no longer make you as happy as you were, not without this individual influencing your life. You love everything about this person. You love the way they look at you, like nobody ever has, you love the way they challenge you like nobody has, and you love the way they love you like nobody ever could. You just cannot imagine spending a moment of your life without this person. You can only hope and wish that you will never have to find out what that's like.

Before you met this person, the whole world revolved around you, and you alone. It was nice when you were on your own. You could do whatever you wanted, whenever you wanted, and however you wanted. Then this person enters your life and they see through your façade; they see you. Everyone wants someone in their life who will vow to fiercely love them now and forever, every bit of them. We all seek that one person who will make that promise to us but it's important to always remember that this love is a once in a lifetime thing. You want someone who understands that, no matter what challenges lie ahead, what obstacles get in the way, they will always be with you, or find a way back to you. We all want to find and hold onto that person at some point in our lives.

Chapter 22

When you meet someone special, they teach you how to let someone in, they teach you how to trust and they teach you how to truly love. This isn't the kind of love some people think they experience every day. It is real love, a love you cannot possibly describe. It makes you see the world like you've never seen it before. You appreciate new things, mostly the people in your life. Nobody in the world is the same. No relationship will ever be the same. Each one is unique. But every relationship is similarly powerful and influential. When you share your life with this someone, you get the opportunity to see the world through their eyes, appreciating more things, including yourself.

What happens when all that is taken away? When, what you thought would once make you whole, is gone. Does it make the feeling of something missing seem even greater?

If you knew what true happiness was, is it much harder to fill again? I think that is the case.

In some cases, when you find that someone who makes you feel whole, something else you may have been looking for gets masked.

But how often is it that someone comes along and covers up what you are really missing?

Is glossing over something another means of filling a void? Is it possible that truly loving relationships can mask something you're missing … that something you believe is missing in your life?

Often relationships, even relationships that lead to years of marriage, do not last the test of time. Yes, there are many that do. Many people are lucky enough to find that person the first time, knowing they will spend the rest of their life with them. It's possible that this person can help them not just cover up what's missing, but also fill that piece in for them. However, most people aren't that lucky.

For some it may require a second, third or fourth person before they find the person who can help them fill that gap. Consider yourself lucky if you are with someone who is able to fill that void for you. In a relationship though, how do you know when enough is enough?

When you believe you are in love, but feel there should be something more. How do you make the decision to move on?

When you are in a relationship there is often more than just yourself to think about, more than just one person who is emotionally involved. When you are with someone for a reasonable length of time, their friends and family become part of the relationship as well.

You have the mother wanting the best for her son, the father wanting to be proud of his strapping young lad, the siblings you get to know and become good friends with, and the friends who look out for their pal and constantly judge and critique you every step of the way … wanting to make sure you are good enough for their friend. There are more people you have to consider, it's not just your own heart.

I'm not sure if there are any break-up rules that we should be aware of. If there are, then they certainly weren't delivered with my mail when they were sent out. After a break-up, should you wait two months, six months, or a year before you speak to them again? Do you need to keep that fake smile in your back pocket in case you accidentally run into someone you were hoping you wouldn't see. I'm not sure who made up these rules, but after a break-up it seems as though everyone is aware of them but you.

Falling in love is hard for anyone. It's the moment when we close our eyes and throw away everything that seems reasonable and vulnerable, and we hope to God that there is someone or something waiting on the other side to catch us. There are only two outcomes: either we are lucky and someone is there to help us, or we wind up bruised on the floor.

Chapter 23

Love can make us do the most extraordinary things. It is the emotion that can lift us up to our highest point, and similarly bring us down to our lowest point.

Love is a scary and dangerous craving, or addiction, to have. It can turn us into people we aren't, people we don't want to be. It can make us feel like we are walking on clouds, but it can also make us feel like hell. It can ruin everything else for you. It can impact decisions you make, actions you take, and the way you think. It doesn't always follow a smooth path.

True love can be felonious. You take someone's breath away, you steal their heart and you rob them of their ability to take a step forward or utter a single word when you're gone. It sounds hurtful, it sounds wrong, yet everyone dreams of experiencing it … of experiencing true love, even if it is just for a short period of time.

We need to make sure that we don't love blindly. Sometimes your feelings could be so strong you could be too much in love, to the point where you don't see the negative impact it has on your life or the lives of those close to you. Yes, do love. Yes, let yourself be consumed by that person you love and never forget why you love them, but never be fooled. In a way I am optimistic though. Love has the ability to leave you with selective amnesia, similar to childbirth I suppose. You completely forget the distress you were in, and how much pain it caused you, until you experience it again, like being in that delivery room again. Sometimes, although we may hope and wish for it, love doesn't conquer all. But it does make things interesting. It does have the ability to boost us, to excite us, and sometimes to heal us to the point where we are willing to shut our eyes, take a deep breath, and jump in again.

It's not always easy though, and very few come out of a relationship unscathed. People may try to cover it up, but every relationship you are in leaves its mark. In some cases, it can halt your journey. That first time, when you wake up after a break-up and don't feel like crying, is when you realise that life is too short, and there are opportunities you are missing.

Break-ups and hurt are inevitable, but you do need to get out there and experience life, love, and everything in between.

If a relationship ends, there is a reason for this. It's probably because there is someone or something out there waiting for you. It is your heart, mind and body letting you know that you are not complete. You feel it as a lack of passion, or sense of purpose. However you feel, it feels wrong.

Love is a major part of life, but it is not everything. There are other aspects that can complete a person and enhance their life.

Chapter 24

I have had many noteworthy conversations with a number of friends and family members, work colleagues, or just individuals who have had some influence on me in my life so far.

They are individuals who I have had the opportunity to meet, people who really do take on life and power their way forward. For them it isn't just a relationship or one individual that will complete them. They look for something more, something a little more suited to themselves and their needs. Some of these people are ambitious, career driven, and would do anything and everything to get to the peak of their profession. Some would say that this is being greedy and single-minded. They would probably think that these people could not be trusted because they prioritised themselves and themselves only. These individuals know what they want in life, and base life around their careers. They know that, by reaching the peak of their career, doing the work, putting in the hours and moving up the ladder, and meeting the right people, will fulfil them. They do care about having a relationship, and the possibility of having a family, but at this point in their life, it is all about their career. They have their goals and spend their time working towards this.

Although there are people who think this level of ambition can be more detrimental than useful, I can honestly say that I have learnt a lot from people like this, and I think I understand them.

For the moment, they know what they want and think they know what it would take to make them feel content. They work hard to reach their goal. I was quite jealous of this. But I can see how having a goal does make your professional life that more interesting and exciting.

I found something similar in my sport. I had my goals and knew where I wanted to be, and what I needed to do to get there. It was easy to plan each year. I knew what I needed to do, what competitions I needed to compete in every month, and how much training I needed to fit in around study, work and rest on a weekly basis. As my goals revolved around my education and sport, I didn't really have much time to think about my career and set appropriate goals for my working life.

I have only just reached that stage in my life where I need to focus more on my career and decide where I want to be, and what I should be working towards.

From others, I have learnt that, in the event something goes wrong with the plans you have made, there are opportunities for you to still set your sights high. Even though you may not realise it right now, you gain as much knowledge as you can from people along the way and keep moving forward. You soak up every opportunity, story and anecdote that you can from those older and wiser than yourself, because you don't know what stage in your life you may need to draw upon these learnings.

If you know what you want, don't stop for anything. Some people view this outlook negatively. However, I think there are very few people who can honestly say they did everything they could, everything in their power, to reach their goals. Many people will look back and realise that they could have done more to achieve their ultimate aim. I really admire people who know what they want, but who don't necessarily have the confidence and fortitude to work towards this goal. Yet they let people know they are working towards it and are proud of that. They are passionate about what they do and what they want. It is very important that you work towards your goal with honesty and integrity. There is no point in working towards something, whether that be a career, a sporting achievement or an educational accolade if you ignore other people's feelings, and step over your friends and colleagues in the process of achieving your objective. I have seen this happen in my short career. Although, in the short term this may take you that one step forward, in the long run, it can only have a negative impact. I would love to have clarity on which path to choose and what I should aim for in life. Perhaps it is an age thing. Whilst I am trying out different career options and finding my way, I probably don't need to have full clarity on what I want. At the age of 25, should I know what I want out of life yet?

Chapter 25

By age 25, Mozart had written over 30 symphonies, John Lennon, as part of The Beatles, released over ten studio albums, and Buddy Holly was dead.

Has everyone paved their paths by the age of 25? I know I haven't. I have a road that I am on now. I have goals I want to achieve over the next year or two, but I couldn't say that where I am and what I am doing now is what I will be doing in five years time. Would anyone really want to know? Would you want to know that where you are at this moment in time is where you'll be in ten years? Or would you prefer the opportunity to search for more, hoping to find something different that could fill in any gaps in your life? Would you like to know where you will be in 20 years time, where you will be living, who you will be with, what you will be doing? Or would you prefer to have the chance to live and experience whatever comes your way? It is likely that you may not be having the most positive or enjoyable of experiences at this point in time. Of course there will be times when you wish you could forget, or wish you could have foreseen and changed a certain moment, but perhaps it is these moments that drive us down the road that is our life. It helps us get to where we are meant to be.

Since gaining this clarity, following my transition from a sporting career to a different professional life, perhaps I will realise that something was missing. Maybe it won't be a person, an event or an outcome, but perhaps it will be in the form of greater clarity of what I want and what I will need to do to achieve it.

Without natural passion and purpose, you start to feel empty. The activities you engage in seem to be little more than routine. You're running on autopilot and not really conscious of what you're doing. Time goes by and you feel as though nothing of any real value has been accomplished. Does having this clarity and direction towards your goal put an end to feeling like you're operating on autopilot? Does it stop the belief that you are just going through life, day-to-day, feeling as though you've not actually accomplished anything relevant?

The people I alluded to earlier tend to agree. They too have experienced a similar feeling of something missing. From conversations with them, it sounds as though they have very similar thoughts and feelings to my own. They felt that, even though they had a destination, had a plan on how to get there, and were working their hardest to achieve that goal, there was still something missing. So, even if someone has full clarity on what they want, sometimes that isn't enough. I understand this completely. Even if you know what you want, there will always be some small niggling doubt. Firstly, there will be an element of doubt surrounding whether you will reach this goal. Secondly, if you do succeed, will it be enough? Will that finally satisfy the craving for completeness, for contentment, for achievement?

For some people, their career is everything. Others know

they want a relationship and a family early on, and therefore restrict their focus on career possibilities unless they find a career that fits in with their dream for a family life.

In my case, a career is a way of making my mark in the world, and therefore it is very important to me. Before I settle down with a family, I want to do something for myself, something I can look back on, something my children can be proud of, something I can be proud of. If this is through my career, then that would be fine.

The relationship you have with children is the only one you don't have to earn or prove yourself to. They arrive into the world knowing nobody, but loving you. They do not care about your past and love you even more every day, even if you sometimes don't deserve it. They are only aware of a future with you. I want to be able to put 100 per cent into my future with them, and to do that, I need to feel proud of myself and have something to offer them.

If you are going to spend time focusing on carving out a career for yourself, think about your aims, your goals and what you what to achieve in life.

When you work in an office everyday, people pass by every minute, they peer in and ask questions. Your posture is a reflection of the shape of your swivel chair in this large building full of people scurrying around, working hard.

This is me, this is where I am. I am working hard and really making a difference in the scheme of things I suppose … but is that enough? Is this, what I am doing now, what I was meant to do, perhaps even supposed to do? Possibly not, but for the time being I'm being challenged and possibly even making a difference to at least one of the billions of people on this earth. If I can do this, I will consider myself successful.

Some believe that success is exclusively a matter of individual merit. What historical evidence is there to support this notion? When you look back through history, at people with extraordinary careers in a range of fields, for example, Bill Gates, The Beatles, Usain Bolt, you find people who are outliers in their field. These people were given a special opportunity to work hard and they seized it. Some of these successful people believe that some goals are worthy enough, even find failure glorious. We only grow when we push ourselves beyond what we already know. To become an outlier, this is what you have to do. Outliers don't shy away from failure, they seize the opportunity with both hands and go with it. Success is not just of their own making, it is a product of the world we exist in.

People toil away at a variety of skills, jobs or talents, hoping to succeed, but the thought of failure resides in the back of their minds. They work on perfecting their craft or practice, while they wait to seize that perfect opportunity, one they can take advantage of. Even without the opportunity presenting itself, these people would survive and still live a long, decent life, with a good career. Instead along comes an opportunity that changes everything.

The bottom line is that, even if you see the opportunities coming, people are rarely prepared for these big moments. Nobody knows when their life is going to change, but it does. However, we are not helpless puppets. The life changing moments will present themselves. We can't change this. It's what you do afterwards that counts. This is when you find out who you are.

It's not a case of these people being smarter than anybody else. It's that they have a skill they've been working on for years, one that suddenly becomes a valuable asset.

Everything we are taught through life suggests that success follows a predictable course. It is the brightest who succeed, and the richest who prosper … but perhaps this isn't always the case. The brightest may not be the only ones who progress. Nor is success simply the sum of the decisions and efforts we make for ourselves. Instead, it is a gift. You can succeed when presented by these opportunities, but you need to have the strength and presence of mind to seize them.

The lesson here is simple. Although it may seem unbelievably easy, it is often overlooked. Some of us often get caught out by the myth that these very successful outliers spring naturally from the earth.

We look at people like Bill Gates, Michael Jordan, and The Beatles, and wonder how the world aided their greatness. Perhaps this perspective is incorrect. Our world gave these people the opportunities to excel, and they seized them. However, if a million children were given the same opportunities, would we have an abundance of amazing musicians, sports athletes and entrepreneurs? Wouldn't it be great if our success, and our futures, were determined purely through seizing these opportunities and working hard at them. Sometimes it is all about being given the chance, the chance to be the person you want to be.

Chapter 26

Our jobs and careers can make a difference, both to ourselves and to others.

But is there a difference between who you are and what you do?

So many people out there, your friends, family, strangers, will associate your job and the work you do with the person you are and the person you hope to be, but there are many factors that contribute towards the career you embark on, the enjoyment you get from it, and the relationship between the effort you put in and the reward you receive.

If you were offered the choice of being a doctor, earning £20,000 a year, or working in a tollbooth every day for the rest of your life for £100,000 a year, which career path would you take?

Off the cuff, I'm sure a lot of people would notice the significant difference in wage and opt for the job in the tollbooth, believing they could handle the monotony, the loneliness, and the repetitive nature of the job. I'm not saying that this is not an important job, not worthy of a good wage or person with great potential. As with all jobs, you need people to do them, or the world would cease to function.

When we take the time to think about it, I guess many people would opt for the former, because of its complexity, autonomy, and the relationship between the effort required and the subsequent rewards. The work is amazing and creative, it helps save lives every day. This alone is more rewarding than the financial gain.

Some people aren't conscious of the relationship between effort and reward, especially when it comes to life. This can be in your career, a relationship, or in perfecting a skill or talent. The longer you work at something, the better you get and the more success there is.

Even if you're on the right track, you'll get run over if you just sit there waiting for something to come to you. As mentioned earlier, when you are work for something, it isn't just about the effort you put into this, it's also about taking the opportunities presented. However, opportunities are often missed by most people because they are sometimes camouflaged when they arise. But hard work will be rewarded.

The link between effort and reward consists of three elements: the connection, autonomy, and complexity. Many agree that in order for work to be satisfying, these three qualities need to exist.

It isn't just about how much money we make, although this can make time spent at work a little more satisfying. It is about how big your office is, or which famous person you get to meet. It is more to do with the satisfaction and fulfilment we get, that keeps us happy between the hours of nine and five, five days a week, forty-six weeks a year. A career that fulfils these three criteria is meaningful to most people. Being a teacher is meaningful, and being a doctor is also meaningful. Hard work can seem like a prison sentence if it doesn't have meaning or satisfaction.

Once a job, a career, or an interest has meaning, it gives you a reason to wake up in the morning and carry on. It makes you want to work hard, improve and succeed. It makes you want to be good at what you do.

This is the case for many jobs, despite variations in culture, pay and status.

Let's take a clothes designer: firstly, there is a clear relationship between effort and reward in this line of work. The harder you work and the more clothes you design, the more money you make. Secondly, the level of complexity involved in the design of clothing is quite intricate. It is not a monotonous career, it varies in detail and learning daily. Thirdly, it is an autonomous line of work. You are not necessarily dictated to or bullied into designing more clothes or better items. It is completely up to you what you do and how committed you are. You are left to go about your own business.

Together these three characteristics make a job meaningful and enjoyable, and subsequently worth persisting with.

This applies to teachers, doctors and even athletes. Usually, the more you train, the better you become. Training may vary day-to-day, with different factors coming into play, but it is up to you to decide how much training you do and when. Nobody is there to tell you what and how to do it. This is something you learn through life.

Seeing your parents and others around you work hard has a knock-on effect. It affects how you see things, and consequently, how you live life.

If you are lucky enough to grow up in a home where

meaningful work is practiced, you begin to learn the lessons that are crucial to those who want to make a mark in life and succeed. If you work hard enough, assert yourself, use your mind and your imagination, you can shape your world to fulfil your hopes, desires and dreams.

Often, to better understand how people who are successful, and potentially outliers in their field or career of choice, are able to reach their pinnacle, you need to look beyond who they are and how hard they work. Some of their success stems from where they came from. Research their family backgrounds, going at least one or two generations back, and focus specifically on what that family has achieved and how they got there. How far you go in life isn't just down to your own efforts, a lot of it is determined by your past and your family.

The "culture of honour" hypothesis states that where you are from is significant, not just in terms of where you grew up or where your parents grew up, but in terms of where your great-grandparents and great-great grandparents grew up. Under this hypothesis, these facts and legacies can and do affect how you act and react to differing situations in your own life.

Sometimes, what you aim for in life, or the level of drive or desire you have, is not directly linked to how confident you are, how bright you are, or how strong you are. Where you come from is a significant influencer.

It has been said that the ability to succeed at what we do is powerfully bound to where we are from. We have to be careful of creating broad stereotypes and generalisations when reflecting on different cultural tendencies and groups. We rarely want to believe that we are prisoners of our histories or culture, but they do affect how we act and what we strive for today.

So, with this in mind, even if we do recognise that there is something missing in our lives, we may not have the opportunity to search and find this missing piece. Perhaps it is out of our control to some degree.

If we haven't grown up in a culture of hard work, with an attitude inclined towards hard work, and the clarity to move forward towards our goals, it's possible that we will never have the opportunity to achieve complete satisfaction, or make that mark in the world that we aspire to.

Chapter 27

What are you going to do with your life? This question presents itself throughout your entire life. It could come from friends, family, colleagues, and teachers. However, it is still a question that never seemed pressing, and I don't seem to be any closer to answering it. The future can rise up ahead of you, in a succession of days, some full, some empty, some fast, and some slow. Each day can be more unexpected and unknown than the previous.

A well-known author once wrote, "the consequences of our actions are so complicated and so diverse that predicting the future is a very difficult business indeed" … it's true.

Once you cut through the obvious, the clutter and the irrelevant, people are pretty much the same as one another, especially during your teenage years and early adult life. For the most part, people will, and often do, go through the same experiences as each other. They often think the same, learn the same things, and perform the same actions. Although, nobody can really escape the belief that their experience is unique in every conceivable way, that our life is our own and that we build it and decorate it in the way we desire. However much you flow with these experiences, you have no way of knowing where you'll end up. You need to put in the effort to reach where you would like to be. Anything that happens along the way will be dealt with and learnt from, but if you have somewhere you would like to be, keep searching for it.

At the age of 25, many people aren't too sure of who they are. It is not often given much thought. You assume that you will marry, have children, and live in a town similar to the one you grew up in. You wouldn't think much different to anyone else you walk past in the street. You're an ordinary person leading an ordinary life, and that may suit you fine. Some are happy living life like this, and are content with people seeing them this way. Some people may not give much thought to it. But for me, this isn't enough. I couldn't be happy with the ordinary. Although, ordinary isn't a word that anyone should be associated with, because an ordinary person doesn't exist in this world. We all have something to offer, something we excel at, something we can teach others. Nobody should settle for ordinary in life, no matter what age they are, or what culture or social status they come from.

Although I have fit a lot into my first 25 years, and have enjoyed every moment, I am curious about what happens between the ages of 25 and 40, the timeframe within which your life plays out supposedly. Plans are supposed to start coming together, you are supposed to begin to get to know yourself a little more, and life is supposed to get a little easier in some ways, harder in others. I'm interested to see whether our expectations lead to disappointment or fulfilment. I am interested in where we end up and how different this is to where we dreamed we'd be. I am also interested in how we got there. I would like to know if we change along the way, from the person we are now to the person we will become.

Do we adapt and grow, or do we continue to cover up cracks when things don't go how we expected or hoped? It is reasonably common for people to get to the age of 25, or around this, and think that they've made it. They think this is who they are and what their life is going to be … but really when you look at it closely, this is just the start. This is an age where you have set foundations and completed the hard grafting. You have studied or learnt a trade, you have worked on securing a group of friends, and have grown closer to your family. You know your likes and dislikes, and you know your needs. At this age, you are starting to figure out what it is you want to be. It should be exciting trying to work out what lies ahead of you. Most start to build a career, other think about settling down and starting a family. You are beginning to get an idea of the person you are and the person you want to be. This is only the start.

You continuously change as a person. Life is full of disappointments, things may not pan out how you thought they would, you may fall in love with the wrong person, you may never have the family life you crave so much, you may not have the chance to get the job you longed for. Does that mean you should be disappointed? No, that's just life. Don't give up, continue to try. Continue living.

The saying "Live each day like it's your last" was probably the most common advice given by many people in your life. In all honesty though, how many of us can manage this. Who has the time and energy, and even the money, to be able to live life this way every day, while trying to keep up with the day-to-day running? Would it not be better to try and just live, to be bold, courageous and confident? Would it not be better to live well, to live right and try and make a difference? You don't have to make a difference to the whole world, that would be pretty tough for most. Perhaps aim to change that small part of the world that revolves around you, the part you are closest to.

You need to go out into the world with your loves and your passions, work hard at what you want, no matter what age you are and no matter what it is you desire. You never know if that something could change your life, or the lives around you.

You should live with passion, live full and live well. Love and be loved, and never hold back because it is what you think you should do. Be brave and try. You carry on living and you continue to surprise yourself. You could also be surprised by what life has to offer.

People live life hoping to meet the expectations and standards of society, friends or family culture, rather than living life the way they want, following their own dreams. There is always pressure on us to live a certain way.

A lot of us fall into the trap of believing that living a life in which you appear to be doing the right things is the same as living a life where you are actually doing what's right for you and you alone. They are not the same thing and cannot be compared.

There are many ways and reasons for pushing yourself further and striving for that extra little bit. Often it is because we think we can do more, need more or that there is more we are missing out on. It's not only ourselves who are the catalysts for this type of thinking and pushing. Our society, our parents and our friends often have a bigger influence on our way of thinking, and personal expectations, than we realise. Society believes that we should grow up, buy a house, meet a partner, get married and have children, in that order. Where did this order originate? Where is it written down that this is the way to go? Why do we need to own a house rather than rent a property, one we are happy in with fewer bills to pay and fewer financial worries? Why should we get married before we have children and start a family? Surely the union of a child together is greater than any sort of union a marriage can create. What can you learn from being married that you couldn't have learnt from being together, living together and loving each other? We all grow up thinking this is the proper route to follow. People put themselves through a lot of trouble to conform to what they believe they should be doing. People conform to what they think their parents want them to do. People conform to what their friends think they should do. People buy these great houses and great cars, they hold great weddings and parties because it is what they believe is expected of them. Often it isn't these things that make you happy though. Happiness does not come from great spending or lavish outlays, it comes from the smaller things in life. There has always been, and always will be, pressure from the greater world we live in.

Chapter 28

For many people in this world, and many I know personally, how they are seen and perceived by the outside world, and by those around them, can often be more important and more influential than their own needs, hopes and aspirations. The presence of this mindset can lead to a culture where a set of ideals does not necessarily reflect what an individual hopes to achieve, where they want to go, and who they want to be. Instead they focus on how they are perceived by the rest of the world.

These ideals largely determine your choices and decisions. These ideals have an impact on who you marry, how many children you have, the type of job you have, the town you live in, the type of house you own, and even the clothes you wear and how much you spend on clothes, cars and presents. Everything in our lives is influenced by these ideals and the expectations of others. But what about what we want? What if we would like to have children out of wedlock? What if we would like to rent instead of owning a house? What if we'd rather spend money on nice food and drink rather than fashionable clothes and expensive cars?

Even when people conform to what is classed as correct and ideal standards, having done things in the right order, with the right family culture and family ways, they find that they are not truly happy. Adhering to all the rules doesn't mean you are truly happy. There will still be something missing.

Family culture and society's ideals often demand that we lead a life we may not be suited to, one we don't actually want. These ideals and cultures can sometimes exert pressures that result in unhappy and unavoidable consequences. This relentless, on-going battle, where we strive to live up to the ideals set by friends and family, ensures that we seem perfect to those around us. But we are often in conflict with our genuine selves, with the genuine ideas and hopes for our own futures. In some cases, we think that we do not live up to certain expectations, subsequently resulting in the need to search for more, sometimes searching for things that may not even be there. Being in conflict with yourself, when you feel as though you've not hit expectations, can leave you in a rut, one you may not be able to pass.

Age makes a major difference in these situations. When you get to a certain age, you know yourself fairly well, and you begin to make decisions that are to your own benefit. You do things and make choices for yourself, not others. When you are younger, and less experienced with your own wants and needs, these internal struggles to satisfy yourself and others can become one-sided and unfair.

Due to years and years of conditioning, mostly from past generations, it is difficult to ignore the expectations set by society, friends and family. Your family and the people around, hugely influence your ability to move away from living by these ideals, to making decisions based on other's expectations. Luckily, I have had people around me who accept me for who I am. My family will accept any decision or choice I make, as long as they are sure I am doing things for the right reasons, for my own happiness. I have met people who have fought against these set ideals and come out the other side more successful, happy and hopeful than ever.

Chapter 29

Perhaps that feeling of something missing comes along when you stop moving forward. You fall into a comfortable slow pace, locked in the same routine with the same people, with the same actions and outcomes. Could it be that one feels as though something is missing when you reach this stagnant state? Does no one feel as though something is missing in their life if it is moving in the right direction? Passion is a key indicator in determining whether what you are doing in your life, the choices you make and the dreams you fulfil, bring you closer to your true self, where you are moving in the direction you want. Passion is the mechanism that supposedly guides us to following the path that suits our own needs best. This feeling doesn't fall short in providing us with the support we need in life when aiming to live up to our own expectations, hopes and dreams. Passion is there to stop us falling short of an accomplishment, or to bring us closer to our true self, desires and needs. It can seem confusing, I know. You can be passionate about things you can only dream of. This alone could take you down a path you would never have imagined embarking on. I believe passion provides the energy required to support the confidence we need to be able to open our eyes and our hearts. It helps us recognise the opportunities available to us and supports us in our next great leap and adventure, where we may find that something missing. It could be that being passionate in life stops us from running from ourselves, allows for a stillness, where we take the time to understand who we are, what we are capable of, and the endless possibilities open to us. It is a journey most of us may have to take at some point in our lives. Consciously or not, we embark on this journey in the hope that it will help pave the road we are heading down. Does having a feeling of something missing in your mind, heart or body highlight that you are not complete, that you cannot give up, or be satisfied with the life you have? It would feel as though you lack passion and miss that sense of purpose, but it can be easily remedied. We all need to feel passionate about something in our lives. As alluded to earlier, this could be anything from a job, family, or a hobby, something that simply has the ability to make you feel better about yourself, something you are willing to spend time on. This kind of passion leads to purpose. Without this natural purpose and passion, you can feel empty. Any activities you partake in can seem as though they are no more than part of your daily routine. You go into autopilot mode and live each day just to get through it, without nothing much different happening. A monotonous existence. Time goes by and you feel as though nothing of any real value stems from your life. However, there is a need to continue living life like this. Where a single action, choice or decision can change how you feel and how you go about your day.

Regaining your passion in life, and for life, and realising that what you do has some value, is essential to fulfilment. It is key for when you begin to understand and search for that something you believe to be missing in your life. When you do establish that something is missing, it is hard to ignore. It screams for your attention, and will continue to do so until you take action. Some deal with this by turning and running away from this realisation. Others seek out relationships or experiences that give them temporary relief, but they continue to evade their feelings, looking for the next distraction. If you keep running though, there will come a day when you hit that wall, where there is no turning back. This is usually the case for someone who is stuck in their familiar routine, one who is dependant on monotony. You may end up as someone you had no intention of becoming, but it will be too late to try and turn things around.

Chapter 30

When people see good, they expect good. Sometimes though, you don't want to live up to anyone's expectations. People may begin to form an idea of you that sometimes isn't quite true. They may see you as the good girl, the safe girl, or the swot. Although, this may not be what you want people to view you as. Perhaps you'd like to add a sense of danger or adventure to stimulate people's perception of you. Of course you want to be a good person, make good choices and be there for your friends and family, but it would be nice to also be able to offer something a little unexpected. A lot of people try out the saying that you should do something new and challenge yourself every day. This is easier said than done when you're living your life, working a job, or looking after a family. But perhaps there is a lesson to be learnt here: unless we push ourselves in certain areas of our lives, we will get stuck in a routine, and the longer we are there, the harder it is to get out.

So if you feel like something is missing, perhaps you need to step inside yourself and find your passion, hopefully it will guide you in the right direction. The day you run out of excuses about changing, about taking chances, about trying something new or following your dreams, will be the day your life changes.

Chapter 31

Have you ever wondered what really marks our time here? Whether one's life, or actions, can really make an impact on the world? Or whether the choices we make actually matter?

I believe they do. I also believe that one person can change many of the lives they encounter along the path they lead, the career they choose, or through their actions alone.

Some people strive for perfection in everything they do, hoping to make more of a difference and fill a gap in the career they pursue or the family they choose to raise.

Some people are lucky in that they grow up knowing exactly what they want to become later in life, and how to achieve this. If they want to become a doctor, they go to medical school; if they want to become a lawyer, they go to law school; if they want to teach, they complete their teacher training. It's easy, right?

You pick your career, you do the required hard work, and then go on to make your mark on the world. You make the difference you set out to achieve, which comes in many shapes and sizes. An impact doesn't always need to involve re-inventing the wheel, or electricity, for that matter. Making your mark could simply come from the act of helping someone pave their own life, making those close to you laugh, helping people lead a happy, fulfilled life. A teacher, for example, makes a difference through teaching children the difference between right and wrong. They help children develop their skills, and sets them onto the right path to making their own mark on the world. A police officer walks the streets, trying to ensure the roads are safe for us and our families, making sure we come to no harm.

You can make a difference to the world in many ways. Doctors save lives, army officers fight for our countries. These are notable careers that have an impact on our lives. However, it's not just frontline professionals who truly make a difference on friends, family and complete strangers.

A young boy may dream of working with cars. He may appreciate their aesthetics, their dynamics, and the way they operate. Just because he isn't fighting crime or saving our country doesn't mean he isn't capable of making a difference. One day, that boy may learn his trade and design a car that is driven all over the world. His impact comes in the form of assisting individuals in their everyday lives, helping them get to their destinations, possibly helping them make their own mark, bringing them closer to achieving their dreams.

A young girl may be interested in clothes from a young age. She may love the creative side with which textures work, what colours match, and have a range of designs in her head. Just because she isn't saving lives doesn't mean she isn't making difference.

This girl may study the different aspects of creative design such as materials, fabrics and general design principles. She may create clothes that inspire people. She could be instrumental in dressing an individual who is going for an interview for their dream job. She may give that person that extra bit of confidence they need when they face the interview panel, or she may help dress a young woman who is going on a first date, potentially contributing to the love of this woman's life falling helplessly in love with her.

See, everyone plays a part in making a difference to the world and impacting people's lives. These may be people you know. The impact could be in the form of being a good parent, brother, sister or friend, helping those around you, or through your creativeness, be it that piece of art or music that inspires someone to make a life changing decision.

The impacts you make often go unnoticed, but they are there. This is why we should never hold back on anything we want to do. Thoughts lead onto purpose; purpose leads to action; actions form habits, and habits decide characters. It is these characters who amend destiny for you and others around you, whom you yourself may have had a tiny impact on.

Is this a measure of our life? Does it depend on what career path choose, or how we impact the lives of those around us, and those we are unaware of?

It has been said that we leave this world the same way we came into it: naked and alone. So if we do leave with nothing, then how do we measure life?

Is it defined by the profession we choose or the people we choose to love? Is it a measure of our accomplishments?

What happens if we fail to succeed in the goals we have set ourselves, or if we've never truly loved? Then what? Can we ever measure up? Or will the quiet desperation of a life filled with want drive us mad?

People are always compared to their friends, family or acquaintances: who has the best job, the biggest house, the flashiest car, or the perfect family …

Does everyone strive for that perfection, wanting to

be the best so people can look at them and say, wow, that person succeeded, that person has really made it?

Success is quoted in the dictionary as

"The accomplishment of an aim or purpose".

So that can mean anything, right? You aim to be the best parent you can be. You raise two beautiful children and that makes you successful.

You aim for a job in London which earns you £50,000 a year, enabling you to live a good life with your own luxuries, and you're surrounded by the people you love. If you can manage this, you are a success.

I have read many studies and literature on what makes someone successful and how one can become one of those "outliers" in life. Whether that be becoming a billionaire, inventing an object that lives on through time forever, or the possession of an extraordinary talent that makes someone stand out. It isn't all down to knowing what you want to become and working hard to get there. Obviously, this plays a large part in becoming successful, but opportunity also plays an important part in this journey.

Albert Einstein once said, "Most people would stop looking when they find the proverbial needle in the haystack. I would continue looking to see if there were other needles".

Albert Einstein rarely spoke of his intelligence, his relationships or work ethic, but he was rather open about his curiosity, claiming that his accomplishments were due to his ability to notice and appreciate the mysteries of everyday life, the simple actions that are often overlooked and taken for granted. He, like many other successful individuals, were driven by their curiosity to search and want more. These characteristics surely lead a person to finding other people, places or actions that they may not have otherwise found. They may learn something new about themselves, or create something that never existed before. It has got to be characteristics like this that drive you to finding that enigmatic hope of fulfilment and contentment, and hopefully happiness.

As human beings we are naturally curious and ambitious. We spend a good part of our lives wanting, wishing, and pursuing. For the most part, that's OK. Curiosity is good, ambition is good, chasing things with honesty and integrity is good, and dreaming is also good. Although, we need to be cautious that our chase doesn't diminish what we already have. We should not forget the goodness we have in our own lives, the world, other lives and other people that we often take for granted. Search, wish and hope, but see, observe and enjoy everything around you simultaneously.

Chapter 32

Before I began researching the aspects and journeys of life, and considering the opinion of others, I was totally certain that I was in the minority. Particularly in terms of the way I viewed life's journeys, based on the things we were expected to do and say and how we should act.

I have always known that my personality was more inclined towards having that perfectionist ideology. It was present throughout my school life, university and my sport. I never did anything half-heartedly. If I put my time and effort into something, I threw myself into it fully, aiming to be the best I could be. I rarely settled for second best. This may reflect the perfectionist in me, or it may be my competitiveness. It could even be unrealistic, but that is how my mind works. Anyone who has grown up with this mindset will find it difficult to change throughout the course of their life.

When I was at college studying for my A-levels, I knew I needed good grades to get into my preferred university. Consequently, I spent most of my free periods doing the extra work needed. I often stayed up in the evening, writing up my notes taken during class, organising them into a neat colour-coded format for ease of reference. Everything had to be perfect. This may sound like I was being a bit of a bore, a swot, a teacher's pet perhaps, but I knew it was what needed to be done. I didn't let it control my life. I still made time for fun, for time with my friends, and for my sports and hobbies. However, I was always conscious of what I needed to do to qualify for my chosen university, so I dedicated my time and organised myself to accomplish what was required. In a way, I was just being proactive. Although, with sport, I was never truly satisfied with my accomplishments. If I won a match by ten points, I told myself that I should have won by 15 points instead. If I was in a practice session and hit 25 of the 30 shots well, I would reflect on the five I missed rather than the 25 I hit well. This was a natural thought process for me. I have always strived for perfection. This trait is good in that I am constantly pushing myself, always wanting more and having the confidence to aim for the top and be better, but it does have its limitations. I'm rarely satisfied, and seldom see my own achievements. This leads onto another question ... what is perfection?

Is perfection in education about all about getting "A" grades in as many subjects as possible, or, in terms of sport, coming in at first place with every one wanting to beat you, or could it be that you're a CEO, the top earner and everyone looks up to you?

Even if you hit these goals, achieving an "A" grade doesn't mean you got every question right; coming in first doesn't mean you will never make mistakes and will win every match going forward; and earning the most doesn't mean you have the greatest knowledge or experience in your field.

So is this perfectionist ideology the right way of thinking?

Yes, if you want to be the best and strive for more, but

only to a certain extent. Surely pure perfection is impossible to achieve, so working towards this becomes counter-productive at some point, right?

Several studies have been conducted on how successful people got to where they are now, and what sets them apart. Research has also looked into that handful of outliers, who truly rise above the rest. A person with an IQ of 140 is considered above average and deemed impressive. Would an individual with an IQ of 170 necessarily have better success in life, have a better job or earn better money, have a bigger house or a faster car, be generally happier? Initially, you would think this to be the case, but after extensive research, it was found that, beyond a score of around 140, the extra 30 points failed to instigate further advantage. So is there really a need to strive for perfection? Perhaps aiming to be great and enjoying the ride to improve yourself is a much more effective journey to embark upon.

Another example of this theory would be in the sport of basketball. OK, you can't become a professional basketball player at five feet and four inches, like myself. Sure you can enjoy playing it as a hobby, but should you wish to try and make a living out it and reach those dizzy heights of sporting stardom, you've got to be a lot taller than five foot and four inches. Most players are a minimum height of six feet and one inch. However, if a player is seven feet tall, does that automatically make them a better player? Considering Michael Jordan, one of the best players in the history of basketball, stood at six feet and five inches, then no, I can't image that those extra few inches would have made him a better player.

What I am trying to illustrate here is that, for each

activity and journey you undertake in life, there will be those ideologies that determine perfection, but this perfection isn't always what is needed or required.

Continuing with the basketball example, ideally the player will be as tall and as fast as possible, with lean muscles and long limbs. But, other variables need to be taken into consideration in order for them to become a good player. If you are not quite as tall as another player, that doesn't mean you are not perfect. There's no reason why someone can't be just as successful, if not better.

So does this mean that striving for perfection is the wrong thing to do? Is aiming for perfection just a decoy? If you strive to fill a gap by trying to be perfect, dedicating a lot of time and effort to reach that ideal, perhaps you are just wasting valuable time, time that could be spent living.

Chapter 33

Stephen King once wrote, "*Time takes it all*".

Maybe this holds true for those who constantly strive for perfection, for those who constantly worry about bettering themselves, aiming to reach for the stars. Perhaps those who sit back, relax and watch their life go by are the ones who enjoy life and inevitably make the most of it. They make the most of what they have and their time on earth.

This is a way of viewing it from another perspective.

I think I know who I am and what I am like. At 25-years-old it would be hard to change the way I am, the decisions I make and the actions I take, even if I wanted to. To be honest though, when I look at things retrospectively, the time that I spent rewriting my notes, neatly colour-coded while I was studying, could have been used to do something else, which may have proved to be more useful and productive. Would this have improved my knowledge and helped me achieve even better grades? At sports competitions, you hear athletes talking about having that positive mental attitude. By focussing on the areas you are weak on in order to improve, you are focussing on the negatives. This can be detrimental to the game overall. So maybe being a perfectionist is a more detrimental personality trait.

I suppose if everyone was aiming for this ideological perfection, then perfection wouldn't be such a great achievement. Perhaps it's better to just let go and be yourself. Accept that you cannot be perfect, but only a perfect version of yourself. This is what you should be aiming for. If you put your all into something, then wherever you go, whatever heights you reach, or status you gain, this will form the perfect version of you.

My parents always said, throughout my studies, sports and work, that you can only do your best. When you are growing up, you tend to take this as something your parents say to make you feel better, to help you relax, settle the nerves and any pressure you may be under. In actual fact, perhaps there is more to this. Maybe if we did accept and trust that trying our best would create the perfect version of ourselves, and being satisfied with this version, could even fill that gap, that feeling of something missing. If you are the perfect version of yourself, what else do you need?

I wanted this book to be perfect, but I now see that perfection is difficult to achieve. Perhaps it isn't everything it's cracked up to be. Everyone is different. They will have different likes and dislikes, and that is a good thing. I have also come to realise that life should be a little messy, that that's how it is supposed to be lived. Therefore, an ideal perfection isn't the best thing to aim for.

Someone's life can often be described, largely remembered, or told as a chronicle of great people doing great things. For most of us though, life is not made up of similar monumental moments. It consists of a series of small moments, some that are important, that can become a story that is significant and overwhelming.

Chapter 34

When writing any story, you form a world that can cover those monumental moments. It has the potential to drive the lives of others. In writing, you can create a world where that short, overweight child becomes a premier league football star; where the girl with braces and bad skin becomes the prom queen; or where the child who didn't perform well at school becomes a city high flyer.

Everyone's life is a story, and it is the heart of language. Everyone's story is emotional in its own way. It moves us to love and to hate. It can motivate us to change the entire course of our lives. A story can lift us beyond our means, our limits and our individuality, to imagine and live the realities of other people, other places and other times. Fiction allows us to empathise and relate to other individuals. To some extent it takes us beyond our own world, into other people's universes.

Every one of us is born with a blank page. It is up to us to form the words that go into the creation of our story, so we are able to leave this life with a full book that tells a great story, one that people would want to read. Some of these stories may be dramatic, some may be horrors, and others may have that happily ever after ending, but you can be certain that each story will be unique to each individual. The story we create is a narrative of our own life and experiences. The stories are not a recount of our daily happenings. They are narratives of what we make happen and what we do with these experiences. We can speak this narrative, write it down or keep it to ourselves, but it is still our story.

We share this world with over seven billion people. Each one of these individuals has their own unique story filling the pages that reflect the creation of their lives and their attempts to make sense of everything.

These distinctive stories help us move in and out of each other's lives. We become a character in someone else's story, before moving back into our own. The story creates and opens up spaces between people who are outside of the reality we live in. By creating and telling our story, we create a world where we are able to invite others in, to experience and enjoy. By listening to other people's stories, we accept the invitation to hear, see and, to some extent, live other people's experiences, which are likely to be different to our own. We can choose whether we want to be part of a story that has the capacity to impact our own.

With every small choice, with every small decision, we are defining ourselves and directing our lives.

Are we proud of ourselves, or are we disappointed by who we've become? Well, it can change. Maybe you are not happy with your actions made in the past or the decisions you made. You may wish you could go back in time and change certain things, but we have got to understand that there is always time to change things. There will always be time to find that something in your life that isn't working, or that isn't making you happy, and correct it.

Regardless of whether you are 20, 50 or 80-years-old,

this concept applies. It is you who makes the decisions, you who inevitably paves your own life. There may be influences you cannot control, but you can deal with these and move on. Life isn't all about hearts and flowers, parties and smiles. It is also about pain and mess, difficulty and confusion, in addition to joy and order. When you allow yourself to realise this, this is the moment when you start to grow up. Although, perhaps people don't ever grow up.

Maybe it's just a cover, just the clay of time to mask the fact that men and women are still children deep down. They want to still jump and play, but that heavy clay of time won't let them. They would like to shake off the chains the world puts round them and return to their old life, their life of freedom, with no responsibilities, even if it's just for one more day. People may like to feel free and secure in the knowledge that their parents are at home, willing to take care of everything and love them unconditionally.

Often, behind the face of the meanest man in the world, there is a scared little boy; similarly, behind the face of a confident business man, there lies an insecure child. I'm fairly certain there are quite a few adults who want to go back to that time where they believed they lived in a magic place, where nothing bad could ever happen. You want to go back to that time and place where everyone was good and kind, a place where hard work was rewarded and people were honest, truthful and willing to help.

Growing up can be a great comfort, but it is also amazingly stifling. As a grown up, there are times when you realise that, perhaps there never was such a place, and perhaps there never will be. But even then, knowing this can't stop you from wishing it could be true.

Life rarely goes the way we planned. The unexpected happens and it surprises us with new and exciting possibilities, which you have to grab with both hands. You don't often know where you are heading, and are unsure about what will bring happiness, or complete your life, until you come across it. It takes us back to that old saying, "I'm looking, but I don't know what I'm looking for. Maybe everything, maybe nothing, but I'll know when I find it".

Sometimes it doesn't matter how you envision life, or how you plan it. Without you even being aware, life has a way of finding exactly what you need, forming you into who you need to be, and sometimes takes you exactly where you need to be.

A lot of people may find themselves sitting on their own one night, or laying in bed one morning thinking, is this it for me? Is this the life I need to be getting on with, the life I will need to learn to love?

Sure you have those moments in your life, where you are on an adventure, where you are excited about the day ahead, where you are challenged, when you feel excited and nervous at the same time. I should also hope that everyone has those times in their life when they enjoy themselves, safe in the knowledge that this is the life for them.

Although, surely everyone has days where they get that feeling in the pit of their stomach, or that nag in the back of their head, where one thinks there is something more, something else that one needs to experience, something else they need to feel.

If we knew we were meant to feel this way, and that there was something that would make this feeling disappear, life would be boring, right? We would have full vision of the future. We would know whether we'd have the family we wanted, the career we wanted, the social life, excitement and adventure in our lives that we craved. If we knew that everything was going to end up how we planned it, then surely the excitement factor would disappear, and life wouldn't be life.

Maybe it's better to have these thoughts and feelings because it means you always have hopes and expectations that something will happen, something that will change your life, that your life will gain momentum, grow and become something that you really didn't expect. Potentially, something unforeseen can occur, which can surprise you for the better and give you something you wouldn't ever have dreamt of having. Something that could make your life even better.

Chapter 35

There is this theory that rolls about from time to time, the theory is about moments, certain moments of impact. I have heard this theory, camouflaged in a number of different forms and scenarios, a few times throughout my life, and again quite recently. I am intrigued by how it sounds, the story you can gain from it and the meaning behind it.

If truth be told, I cannot categorically state what this saying means. I suppose it is one of those sentences or scenarios that holds its own meaning for each and every individual. The definition and the feeling it gives is moulded by the personality it comes from. This is what often differentiates the paths we all take, the outlooks and goals.

The theory is that the moments of impact, those flashes of high intensity that completely turn our lives upside down, usually end up defining who we are and who we become. The formula is simple in that we are the sum of every moment we've ever experienced, and the people we've ever known. It's these moments that shape us and form our history. It creates our own greatest hits of memories, ones that play over and over again. Even one moment of impact can make a difference. One moment of impact that has potential to change with rippling effects, over and above what we predict. It is when some of these particles come crashing together, bringing some closer together than before while sending other particles spinning off into the beyond, to somewhere where you can't imagine finding them, or even imagine them going.

That's the thing about these moments, you can't, no matter how hard you try, control the affect they have on you and those around you. You just have to let the colliding particles land where they will, and wait, until the next collision takes place.

For me these moments of impact represent moments of passion and inspiration, times that people use for their inspirational songwriting, powerful photography or passionate speeches.

Often the people around you are the inspiration, and therefore it is these people who create moments of impact for you … I know this is the case for myself.

You can get inspiration from people you meet for the first time, but most moments of impact come from the people who are in your life daily. It is these people who have the capacity to make their way into your heart and make an impact on you, and often your life. They can make you angry or sad, but they can also make you the happiest you have ever been. Most of all, they have the power to make you stop, wonder and think, which only makes you grow as a person.

All these people who flow in and out of your life have the capacity to change it. It does change you in one way or another. You may not be aware of it though.

Sometimes the end result can have negative implications, but from what I have learnt so far, every impact will leave a positive imprint on your life.

I have become who I am today because of every single person in my life, and because of every single impact and event. People turn out the way they are because of their experiences, their stories and their adventures. They have grown into that individual, influenced by who they have met throughout their lives and what they have seen. This in turn influences a person's behaviour, actions and intentions.

Sometimes we get so caught up in our own moments of impacts, we forget about other people's impacts. If you take the time to understand other's reasonings, decisions and actions, you will begin to understand their stories and their lives. If you're lucky perhaps, you may even start to gain an understanding of how this world we live in works.

This is what separates a truly compassionate, understanding and educated person from many others around us.

When we combine our moments of impact and our stories with those around us, we learn, we understand, and we share.

However, we often let these moments pass us by without a thought. We don't always think about the consequences. If they were taken away from you, or if you couldn't remember them, would you change as a person? How would your life and the people around you change?

Whilst writing this book, I slowly began to understand. You can let go of the negativity and regrets that you may have held on to, making room for more moments of impact, more adventures and greater changes in your life.

Your life will be full of moments. Some of these we will wish had never happened, some we will wish we could freeze in time and keep with us forever, others act as the bridge to move us onto the next moment; there are too many moments to list them all.

Life is full of these moments. It frequently makes me wonder how we are able to remember the details of the more significant moments. Yet we find it hard to remember a conversation we had ten minutes ago or we sometimes forget why we walked into a room.

Family moments, partner moments and friendship moments are usually those that are difficult to forget. Happy or sad, they often stick around.

Although some of these moments are excruciatingly tough and painful, they are still moments you are blessed with. This may sound mad, but being hurt, sad or conflicted defines the person you are today. You need to cherish these moments. They change you in ways you could never imagine. They give you strength, and as my dad would say, they build character. Although some would laugh at that saying, I have realised just how true it is.

Chapter 36

Life carries on. The paths always lead to unexpected destinations. That is the beauty of it all: not knowing what we want or where we are going. We are born with this uncertainty and, as children, it's what we thrive on through adventures, magic and the unknown. Through trying things for the first time. So why do we all have the urgency to lose this experience?

Time can feel different when you are a child, as you are still growing up and finding your feet … it always feels like there is a lot of it, like time will never run out, or that your life seems to go on forever. Don't be in a hurry to grow up. Hold on to being young for as long as possible. Once you lose the magic that only young people have, you will find yourself searching everywhere to find it again, often an impossible feat.

We all start out knowing magic, we are born with it. It is the magic of being given life, that we have become part of our family through our creation. This magic pops up whenever, no matter how briefly, it does manifest itself. When people get weepy during films, it's because, in that dark cinema, that magic was sparked for just a moment, just briefly. Then they emerge into the soft sun of logic and reality, the magic is gone, just as quickly as it appeared. When a song stirs a memory, when you hear the rain pattering on the window, when specks of dust pass through a shard of light, it takes your attention from the world. When you see a plane overhead, you wonder where it's going, you step beyond where you are and move into the realms of magic, where anything is possible.

Every year we grow, we move further and further away from the essence of magic we are born with. We get shouldered with burdens, get sucked up into the routine of life's experiences. Some are good, others aren't. Life itself does its best to take that memory of magic away from us every day. You aren't always aware of it until you wake up one day, feeling as though you have lost something, lost a much needed part of you, but you're not sure what that is. You need the memory of magic to conjure it up again, and to ensure that life doesn't completely ruin the essence you were born with.

Surely the key to forming a life you are happy with, can be excited about, and can see yourself living for the rest of your life, one you feel satisfied and complete with, is to find this magic you were born with, and hold onto it. Keep on believing that if you really want something, go and get it. You need to follow the saying: "to have the serenity to accept the things you cannot change, the courage to change the things you can, and the wisdom to know the difference". You need to know what you can have in your life and what you need to change to be able to make life worthy of you. With this though, you need to realise that there are parts of life, necessities that come to everyone, that may not be enjoyable or what you hoped for. Everyone will experience a break-up, stressful times at school or work, and general down days, when they believe they could be doing more. However, it is self indulgent for you not to appreciate what you have. When someone weighs up what they have against the things they would change, I am sure most people would come to the same conclusion.

Chapter 37

So what happens when it's all over, when our time comes to an end?

I suppose it's a similar thought to wondering how we got here in the first place?

If you forget the tales of Adam and Eve, which I'm a little unsure about anyway, how did we end up in the place we are in and the people we are with? Some people like the myth of the Pawnee Indians, who believe that the star deities populated the world. The evening star and the morning star got together and gave birth to the first female. The first boy came from the sun and the moon. Then there are the scientific theories about natural gases mixing with carbon matter, which subsequently solidified into an organism and started the evolutionary chain. The amazing thing is that, no matter what you believe, it took some doing to get from the point where there was nothing, to a point where all of the right cells fire up so we can make decisions on who we are and where we go.

It is a similar wonder what happens afterwards and where we go from here.

I have often wondered whether there is a difference between what happens when we are ready to leave or if we unexpectedly leave this life and move on to the next? Will there be an opportunity in the next life to achieve that completeness or does happiness prevail when it is all over? I believe in a higher power, but I am not sure who or what this higher power is or what it can do. If we were to leave before we had the chance to live our lives fully, perhaps we would reach somewhere where we could look over our loved ones and help guide them and protect them, ensuring they were OK without us. We hope we can help them live their lives in the best way possible, perhaps even guide them to where they need to be.

If you have lived your life and your time is up, when nature decides it's time for you to go, I would like to believe that that is the end. You would have lived your life, but it is now time for someone else to live theirs. You can leave knowing that you have lived a full life, provided happiness, guidance and joy to friends, family and sometimes even to strangers, who may have simply benefitted from a smile you gave them or a door you held open. Perhaps the knowledge of your journey and the changes you have made can create the true contentment and happiness one desires.

You will always have memories of that life. The flow of voices and the tiny, insignificant day-to-day make up the memory of living, and it is often these things that are never forgotten. Some say that the stars are holes in heaven, and that every time we see the people we love shine through, we know they are happy.

However, considering all the pain and unfairness that surrounds certain instances, and the varying degrees of luck, the thought of there being a higher entity doesn't quite fit. Perhaps there is nothing that creates and directs our lives.

Perhaps only our loved ones can help us through life. There will be moments in your life when you will lose someone you love. You may have someone you miss dearly, someone you will miss for the rest of your life. In these instances, the hardest part of saying goodbye is having to do it every single day.

I thought I knew what death was. It has existed in my life for as long as I can remember, from those moments I sat in front of the television, or the huge cinema screen with my popcorn. I must have seen hundreds of fictional characters meet their end in films, soaps and dramas. I thought this gave me a better understanding of death, but I was wrong, because the experience of death cannot be simulated. It cannot be befriended or understood. If death was a person, it would be a lonely figure, always on the outskirts, walking alone, never interacting.

You may think you know death, and be prepared for it. But when someone who is close to you goes, that's when you realise you weren't prepared. Whether you are a doctor, a high flying businessman, a postman or a baker; whether you are old, young, strong or weak, it is the most difficult thing you will ever experience in your life. However, we all have to face death at some point in our lives. Some are lucky enough to go many years without experiencing this, some go through it at quite a young age. No matter when it happens though, you are never fully prepared. You can be the most extroverted and confident person on earth, but talking at a loved one's funeral, or just saying goodbye to someone, will be the hardest thing you will ever do … and this comes from experience.

It is difficult to live in this world of ours. Every day we face the same truths, that life is fleeting, that our time here is short, that we must honour those gone, and we must love our own lives well.

You don't get to choose how you are going to die, where you will go next and when. You can only choose how you live … now. I believe that we sometimes waste words and moments. We don't take the time to verbalise what is on our minds, in our thoughts, and in our hearts, when we have the opportunity to.

The important thing is to remember everything and anything. You shouldn't go a day not remembering a part of it. Store those memories away like a treasure worth millions, because it is.

When you see something, don't just look at it, really see it. When you listen to something, really hear it. Make sure you pay enough attention to be able to truly describe it; write it down for others to experience.

Everything we see or interact with begins with somebody, a friend, family member, or even a stranger, wanting to tell a story. This story may be fact or fiction, but it is a story. It has a beginning, a middle, and an end. It reflects the need and desire to share something.

To plug into a universal socket is probably one of our greatest desires in life. It represents the opportunity to hear stories and live the lives of others for the briefest of moments, making that magic come alive in our bones, creating that excitement for us each day. It is also easier to walk through life with your eyes shut and your ears closed. People will live through a parade of wonders, but they may never live to tell their stories and pass on their amazements. That is a travesty.

Chapter 38

Considering all the areas I have talked about, including key aspects of my life and other people's lives, what conclusions can we draw from analysing the thoughts raised? What revelations, insights or inspirations have I learnt? Perhaps these could help me find that elusive formula for happiness, success or even just satisfaction.

I am sure that when you ask most people what they want in life, some may respond with fame, fortune, family, and health, but the majority would say they just want "to be happy".

Most would view the happiness of their children, friends and family as being more important than wealth, wisdom or success. Despite this, a lot of people in this world spend a huge proportion of their lives searching for this elusive happiness, to be able to fill that void, that something missing in their lives. It has resulted in the formation of this giant, multi-million pound industry of self-improvement, therapy and motivational talks, but has anyone ever really sat back and thought about whether happiness is truly the goal we should be consistently seeking? Is it a truly achievable goal? Is the idea of happiness sold to us at an early age? Are we led to believe that happiness is the most important thing in life? While we focus on finding happiness, we often lose sight of the complexity and amazement of life and living. We ignore other important pieces of the puzzle in the process of trying to find this one piece.

So can anyone truly be 100 per cent happy, satisfied and content?

Does everyone feel as though they have that something missing, something they can't quite identify? And if so, how do we find it?

To be honest, even after breaking down the lives of the people I have been fortunate to know, I don't know if I am any closer to finding the answer to the questions I have posed. Questions I am sure many others will continue to ask themselves throughout their lives. Perhaps having some sort of belief or faith system would provide the answer to some of these questions. There's a possibility that there are people out there who are completely happy, content and satisfied. People who never feel the need to ask themselves these questions. For me though, these questions exist, will always exists, and will always be important. However,

when you really think about your life, explaining your beliefs may not be that simple. If you say that you believe in something, that it's true, perhaps you are referring to something different?

It may be that you are still weighing the alternatives and therefore haven't yet abandoned the idea, or that you accept it as a fact and agree with the premise. Personally, I don't see the logic and sense in how this one belief can have a variety of contradictory definitions. In reality, and emotionally, it's pretty clear though. There are several instances in life when you think you are doing the right thing, then someone makes you second guess yourself every step of the way. There's not much you can do about this. It happen to us all, big or small, old or young. I still haven't managed to figure out this whole faith thing. Many say that you are supposed to have it, but for this to be true, you need something to have faith in. Some people are just too lost to know what this is.

What if faith is what you are trying to find? What if this is that something missing? What if faith is like talking on the phone with nobody on the other end of the line? It could make you go crazy: asking questions, being unsure whether anyone will reply, but still wishing and hoping that what you are doing is the right thing for yourself, and that it's taking you in the right direction.

Wherever you travel, and whatever you end up doing, there will be people who claim to have all of the answers. I don't know whether this is anything to do with their faith or belief, or whether they are just people with greater insight and understanding. In a way, I am trying to be like one of these people now, but regardless of what people tried to tell me, I chose the route of taking everything as it comes, only believing and understanding something I have experienced. However, the beliefs, faith and insights that these individuals have seem to give them the assurance to speak or write confidently, and that can seem self-justifying and potentially true.

Although, you could pose the same question to a hundred different people, from a hundred different walks of life, and get a hundred different answers. Some will be obvious and have clarity, some may be a little more exaggerated or creative, other responses would be ones you would never have imagined, but they are all valid responses and illustrate that some things are beyond our understanding.

There are so many theories, beliefs, faiths, and explanations.

Likewise, there are so many opinions, thoughts, hopes and understandings in this world. You listen, observe and support, but it is up to you to decide how you feel, how you think and the actions you take. It is your mind and it is your life. You rely on yourself to live it.

The only theory or belief I will always fall back on is my favourite quote of all time.

I would be lying if I said it had got me through some hard times and if I said it had the answers to all my questions, but writing this book has led me back to this quote:

"Whatever you do in life will be insignificant, but it's very important that you do it, because nobody else will."

I think I agree now. Just live well.

.

Printed in Great Britain
by Amazon